# OUT OF THE TIGER'S MOUTH

# OUT OF
# THE TIGER'S MOUTH

## THE AUTOBIOGRAPHY
## OF
## DR. CHARLES H. CHAO

CHRISTIAN FOCUS PUBLICATIONS

© 1991 Charles H. Chao
ISBN 1 876 676 592


Published by
Christian Focus Publications Ltd
Geanies House, Fearn IV20 1TW
Ross-shire, Scotland, UK.

Printed and bound in Great Britain
by Cox & Wyman Ltd, Reading

Cover design
by
Seoris McGillivray

# CONTENTS

I dedicate this book
to the memory of
my beloved Mother,
CHAO LIU TO-CHIA
(Mrs. Dorcas Chao)

## MILESTONES - DR. CHARLES H. CHAO

1916     Born at Changku, Manchuria.

1931     Japanese invade Manchuria.

1932     Marries Pearl.

1934     Samuel Boyle goes as missionary to South China.

1935     Converted under Wang Ming Tao

1936     Began at Yingkou Bible Institute.
        Theodore born (5th. September)

1938     Introduced to Dr. J. G. Vos and to the Reformed Faith.
        Jonathan born (22nd. August)

1940     Called to assist Dr. Vos at Yingkou Bible Institute.
        Helen born (9th. February)

1941     Jean born (3rd. September)

1942     Yingkou Bible Institute closed by Japanese.
        Appointed associate pastor of the Tashihchiao Presbyterian Church.

1943   Sam born (10th. May)

1945   Japan surrenders.
       Russian troops invade Manchuria.
       Harry born (9th. February)

1947   Bill born (20th. August)

1948   Escapes with family to Shanghai.
       Arrives in Canton, South China.

1949   The Peoples' Republic of China.
       Formation of The Reformation Translation Fellow-
       ship.
       Publication of magazine *Reformation Faith*.

1950   R.T.F. work endorsed by Reformed Presbyterian
       Synod of North America.
       Moves to Japan.
       Grace born (12th. September)

1952   Lois born (4th. March)

1953   Rose born (13th. June)

1954   Ordained as minister of Reformed Presbyterian
       Church of North America.
       British Committee of R.T.F. formed.

1956    Graduates from Kwansei Gakuin University. Arrives in U.S.A. to study at Reformed Presbyterian Seminary, Pittsburgh.

1958    Family arrive in U.S.A.

1968    Moves to Taiwan to establish R.T.F. office.

1977    Awarded Honorary Doctorate of Divinity at Geneva College.

1982    Golden Wedding of Charles and Pearl.

# ACKNOWLEDGEMENTS

It was beyond my dreams that I might publish a book in English in my lifetime. Therefore I wish to express my sincere thanks and deep appreciation to my life-long colleague in the translation work of the R.T.F. - Dr. Samuel E. Boyle - for editing the English translation of my Chinese autobiography, *His Grace Abounding*. Dr. Boyle insists that it could never have done his part if Rev. John Wong of Hong Kong had not first translated the original Chinese into English.

I am most grateful to Dr. Loraine Boettner for reading the original English translation by Mr. Wong, and making suggestions to Dr. Boyle for revisions. I am also greatly indebted to Dr. Boettner for writing the Foreword to the English edition.

For her typing of the final draft of the English manuscript, my thanks go to Dr. Boyle's daughter-in-law, Mrs. Carol Boyle. I am also grateful to Mr. Duncan Gordon of Fortrose, Scotland for finally editing the text.

The greatest debt of all, however, I owe to my wife, Pearl, to my sons, Ted, Jon, Sam, Harry and Bill, to Francis Lew, my son-in-law, and to daughters, Helen, Jean, Grace, Lois and Rose. Without their co-operation and assistance the publication of this book would have been impossible.

Charles H. Chao

# FOREWORD

It is with special pleasure that I attempt to narrate something concerning my contacts with Dr. Charles H Chao and his extensive translation work for more than forty years.

My first contact with Mr. Chao was through correspondence with him in 1941, when he was at Newchang Bible Seminary in Yingkou, Manchuria. A Princeton Seminary classmate and friend of mine, Rev. J. G. Vos, had gone to Manchuria as a missionary under the Reformed Presbyterian (Covenanter) Church in 1931, and later was transferred to the Yingkou Bible Seminary, first as teacher of systematic theology and later as the principal. Charles H. Chao was one of his students. Some years before this I had sent Mr. Vos copies of my books, one on the subject of *Predestination*, and a smaller one on *The Inspiration of the Scriptures*. Mr. Vos had shown these to Mr. Chao, and almost immediately he was eager to translate the latter into Chinese. Even at that time Mr. Chao had a strong desire to study in America at some Reformed seminary.

Yingkou Bible Seminary was twice closed by Manchukuo and Japanese military authorities.

When the first government order to close arrived in 1940, its founder and Principal, Mr. James McCommon, had to return to Ireland, so he turned the closed seminary over to the American missionary teachers, including Mr. J. G. Vos. They chose Mr. Vos to be the Principal.

At that time Charles H. Chao had already graduated, and was working in north Manchuria. Mr. Vos wrote to him at once, asking him to return to his alma mater to help as secretary to the Principal. The seminary faculty decided to re-open the Yingkou Bible Seminary, and served notice to various authorities. Charles Chao had the responsibility of delivering this notice to the officials. The school was re-opened in September 1940, but in a short time the local officials closed it for the second time.

At this period things were becoming increasingly tense internationally, so Rev. J. G. Vos and family returned to America in March 1941. Mr. Vos asked Charles Chao to take sole responsibility as caretaker of the seminary property and campus. After the bombing of Pearl Harbor by Japan and the beginning of the Pacific War, Japanese authorities in Yingkou confiscated the seminary buildings and land as enemy property. Mr. Chao was out of work.

A minister who had been his teacher in Yingkou

Seminary kindly introduced Charles Chao to a Presbyterian Church in Tashihchiao which needed an associate pastor, and so the Chao family were able to move immediately to serve in that church. When the Japanese nation surrendered in 1945 and the Pacific War ended, the Soviet Russian armies invaded Manchuria before the American and Nationalist Chinese troops could occupy that area.

Once again war conditions overtook the Chinese in this Manchurian battleground. The Chao family was harassed by Soviet Russian troops, and a rising threat from the Communist Chinese armies built up rapidly. In those dangerous and trying days Mr. Chao was personally endangered by the Communist Chinese soldiers who occupied their home town of Chungku, Manchuria. After a narrow escape from imprisonment and possibly from death, Mr. Chao had to flee to Mukden and for a time leave Mrs. Chao and the seven children in Chungku. These exciting adventures are related in detail in Mr. Chao's story.

I continued to correspond with Mr. Chao as much as possible, giving him such encouragement as I could. While the Chao family was going through these harrowing experiences, I was visited in my home in Washington D.C. one summer evening in 1947 by Mr. Samuel E. Boyle. He was a friend of Mr. J. G. Vos and himself a Reformed Presbyterian missionary on furlough from South China. He had worked for seven years in the southern Province of Kwangtung, around the city of Canton, where he had seen a great need for evangelical and Reformed literature in the Chinese language. He was wondering if a project of some kind might be worked out to translate some of our Reformed theological books for Chinese readers.

In the course of our conversation, I told Mr. Boyle of my contact with Mr. Chao, who had already manifested a strong desire to translate such works into Chinese, and of how Mr. Chao was highly recommended by Mr. Vos as a capable linguist. I gave him Charles Chao's address in Shanghai and suggested that he try to meet him personally. On his return to Canton in 1947, Mr. Boyle wrote to Mr. Chao and arranged for him and his family to move to Canton, South China, where they arrived late in December 1948.

Their meeting and that of their families was a most happy one, and from the very beginning they seemed to work together in almost perfect harmony. There in Canton, with Mr. Vos' assistance, they formed a voluntary faith work called the Reformation Translation Fellowship. From that humble beginning, with each of those three men playing a key part, the Fellowship has developed into the present extensive project that it now is.

The Reformation Translation Fellowship was launched in Canton, China, and moved later to Hong Kong, firm in the belief that, while military and political governments would come and go, 'God's Word is not bound'. The translation and preparation of Chinese books and pamphlets which were soundly Reformed would meet the future needs of the Chinese Christians inside and outside Communist China.

One of the first things which Mr. Chao did was to establish a monthly magazine, *Reformed Faith and Life*. Numerous articles from Reformed writers were translated and published, together with editorials bearing on the conditions of the Chinese churches at that time. The magazine was directed primarily to the churches, seminaries, church leaders and theological students and has continued to grow in circulation. With editorial offices first in Hong Kong, then in Taiwan, *Faith and Life* has gone to Chinese readers in many nations outside China.

The Reformation Translation Fellowship has published nearly seventy books setting forth the Calvinistic or Reformed position, as well as many shorter booklets and articles. All of this has been developed with the conviction that Christianity reaches its most Biblical and fullest expression in the Reformed Faith.

Mainland China today has more than a billion people: that is over four times the population of the United States or of Russia. By virtue of its population alone, China is the greatest mission field in the world. During the past thirty-five years she has been virtually a closed mission field so far as foreign missionary work is concerned. But there are signs that some of the restrictions are now being lifted and that a better day is dawning.

One result of Communist occupation has been the unification of the language of the nation to an extent greater than ever. The official Mandarin or Peking dialect had been the national language under previous governments, but today the enforcement of standard Chinese and the down-grading of local dialects is more successful. This will greatly facilitate the rapid spread of the Christian gospel inside China whenever God removes the present hindrances to evangelism by the churches there.

We are grateful to God for the work that under his providential guidance the Reformation Translation Fellowship has been able to accomplish in putting Reformed literature into the hands of the Chinese people. We hope that in the years to come a strong Reformed church will develop in China.

In all of this, I want to acknowledge Dr. Charles H. Chao, a man of God and the one man who, by his untiring devotion, has been primarily responsible for this development through the years.

Loraine Boettner

# 1

*'Neither are your ways my ways,' says the Lord*
*(Isaiah 55:8)*

It was during a New Year holiday period that my grandfather, a farmer, was playing cards with some friends. One of them turned out to be a rascal: he insisted after the game that Grandfather pay him a hundred strings of 'cash' which he claimed was owed to him because Grandfather had lost.

'Are you serious?' asked my grandfather. A hundred strings of cash was a large sum in those days and he refused to pay. After that, this man came frequently to our house trying to collect the money, and my family suffered much under his continual harassment. Somebody suggested that in order to get rid of him, my grandfather should go to the county seat, Kaiyuan City, and talk to the foreign missionary at the Christian church.

Due to the narrow-minded indifference of the people in Manchuria in those days, the Christian missionaries had difficulty in spreading the gospel. The missionary at the Scottish Presbyterian

Church was delighted to have my grandfather come to him without an invitation, and after that he often came to visit us to preach Christianity. Sometimes he held evangelistic meetings in our village home. The presence of the western missionary really solved my grandfather's problem. His enemy never came again to claim payment of the gambling debt.

Thus, because of the efforts of this unrighteous creditor to collect that debt from my grandfather, God brought the gospel of Jesus Christ to our family.

## 2

*Do not forsake your mother's teachings*
*(Proverbs 1:8)*

I was born on the second of August 1916, the youngest of a family of six. My father, originally a farmer, later became a merchant, and after a few decades of up-and-downs our family had become fairly well-to-do, so we purchased a plot of land. My eldest brother was a farmer, the second became a teacher and the third opened a shop in Kaiyuan City. My other brother and I, being the youngest, were sent to school.

My mother had come into contact with Christianity at the age of twenty-eight. Both my grandparents had known how to read, but they showed little interest in the gospel. In retrospect I now see that my grandfather showed an interest in Christianity only for the sake of expediency. It was the grace of God, however, which brought Christianity to our home through my mother's conversion. Such is God's sovereign plan, for his grace came to me and to my mother, yet it did nothing for all my older brothers and sisters.

From the year I was born our family fortunes began to slide downhill. The problem began with my father's long-cherished desire to take a concubine. He was never serious about religion, so he cherished these lustful desires as his wealth accumulated. My mother committed the problem to the Lord without arguing against my father's plan. Nevertheless, he took a concubine and with three married sons in the family, his action caused him to lose all his authority. After eight more years of this domestic confusion, the family decided to divide the property and split up. I was only eight at the time.

With the exception of my mother, all the rest of the family were indifferent to Christianity. They were jealous of me: I remember that they called me the 'lucky getter'. According to Manchurian custom, whenever a family divided up, the eldest brother who had presumably worked the hardest and had a family of his own, usually got the largest share of the wealth. I, the child of eight who had done nothing for the family, also received my share of the family property; this intensified their jealousy. After the land was divided, we drew lots for the houses. I got the best house of all! Into it my mother took her two youngest sons to live with her.

My mother took special care of me from my

birth, possibly because I was her youngest child. As far back as I can remember I learned to pray and recite Bible verses. I memorised the Lord's Prayer, the Ten Commandments, the Beatitudes and many other Bible verses. I remember that I often went to church on the Lord's Day with my mother. She would take me to a church meeting in some house in our area. I remember that she taught me to greet people, 'Peace to you'. This word 'peace' left an indelible impression on me as a child.

In those days, most preachers liked to preach from the New Testament. I can still recall sermons I heard at those services, such as Jesus walking on the water or Jesus feeding the multitude with five loaves and two fishes. The first book which I encountered before going to school was the Bible. Although I could not yet read a single word in it, I turned the Bible over and over; but the only thing in it which drew my attention was the colourful pages at the end - the coloured maps. But when I started at school I began to learn to read the Bible. Thus the grace of God came to me through my Christian mother who nurtured me with religious instruction early in my childhood.

After I became a teenager I often did things which worried my mother. I loved to fish in the river during the summer, where I could forget all about time. My mother accompanied by a neighbour would come out of the village looking for me. When she found me she would scold me and charge me never to do it again. During those days there were many bandits running about in the countryside who would often hide in the sorghum fields. These robbers would inquire about the rich people in the villages and sometimes kidnap a child of a wealthy family for ransom. This danger frightened all the villagers so that they would not allow their children to run about in the open fields outside the villages.

In our village there was a family by the surname of Hei who had a child just a little older than I. One day this lad went to the sorghum field and came upon some bandits hiding there. Fearing that the boy might reveal their whereabouts the bandits held him prisoner. In the evening, they took him with them when they entered a villager's home and forced the family to cook a pot of rice for them. Then they forced the Hei boy to carry that hot kettle of rice on his back as they fled away. The boy's back was seriously burned by the heat of the rice pot, and he died soon after this from his burns. My mother was afraid that something like that might happen to me, so she made me promise never to leave the village without telling her.

## 3

*May you rejoice with the wife of your youth*
(Proverbs 5:18)

I was engaged when I was fourteen years old. The matchmaker was a neighbour, the uncle of my wife-to-be. We called him Uncle Chang. He was a worker on the Southern Manchuria Railroad under the Japanese, a strongly-built man with a kind and humorous character. All public events like weddings and funerals in our country area were under his voluntary direction and care. One day he said that he wanted to engage me to the daughter of his brother-in-law who worked in an iron factory. Later they came to our house to 'look at' me.

My mother was very open-minded in this matter. She wanted me also to have a look at my possible wife-to-be, so, accompanied by a cousin, I went to meet her. On my return my mother asked me my opinion of her and I said, 'Not bad.' When the girl returned to her home and was asked her opinion of me she said, 'Not bad.' So, with two 'not bads' our lives were sealed together!

Chinese Christians in those days were often unaware of the Bible's command to Christians to marry only Christians. My mother did not know, so she innocently allowed me to marry a girl from a Buddhist home. Even so, God in his wisdom permitted this to happen and worked it out for good.

On September 18th, 1931, there occurred what may be considered the saddest event in Chinese history: Japanese armed forces invaded Manchuria. In my first year of junior high school I realised the weakness of China's national defences. Posters showing our national humiliation by Japan were hung on the walls of all classrooms.

My young heart was greatly distressed by the shame which my country now bore. I remember that on the day of the invasion a few Japanese soldiers entered our school. The first thing they did was to tear down and destroy all the patriotic posters. Then they collected all the textbooks based on Sun Yat Sen's *Three Principles of the People* and carried these away in sacks. The following day all classes were suspended.

I was terribly afraid of the Japanese. I did not dare travel by train, so I hired a horse-cart to carry my baggage thirty miles home. My heart was filled with inexpressible anger and sadness as I returned home with my dreams of an education shattered, and that anger was intensified by the violence which Japanese soldiers were inflicting on Chinese people as they advanced. Banditry sprang up in many places, and people's lives were threatened.

And so it was with the agreement of parents on both sides that we hurried up the wedding ceremony to March 4th, 1932. I was only sixteen. According to Manchurian custom, the wedding date must be set by a diviner in accordance with the exact year, month, day and hour of the birth of both bride and groom. The bride must wear a 'lucky gown', plus a demon-exorcising mirror dangling at her shoulder, and a veil covering her head. These decorations make her look more like a monster than a beauty!

Since our wedding was administered by an elder of the Christian church, all these pagan bridal ornaments were waived. Our wedding was performed with Bible reading and prayers and the singing of hymns. After we were married, it was thought not safe to remain in the rural area and so we moved to Kaiyuan City. Having been influenced by the church, my mother was much enlightened, so she sent my wife to study at the Kaiyuan Bible Institute. We thank the Lord that during these years of study in the Bible Institute my wife came to understand many Biblical doctrines.

Later, she became a believer in the Lord Jesus, and in 1933 was baptized into membership of the Presbyterian Church.

After our family split up, most of my brothers started their own households. When my brother, who lived with my mother and me, married, his wife did not wish to live with our mother, so she persuaded my brother to move out. The reason for this was that my mother corrected her, often telling her daughter-in-law to be more careful with food or to do this or that. The girl was not accustomed to obey, so she rebelled. This left me as the only one living with our mother.

My mother had a secret fear that my wife would also hate to live in the same house with her. I thank God that nothing like that came to pass. They had a harmonious relationship in our home. There was nothing that my mother would not talk about with my wife, even about family quarrels of the past. In fact, my wife was the only one she would speak to about such things.

## 4

*He put a new song in my mouth*
*(Psalm 40:3)*

By this time I had transferred to Kaiyuan County High School. I went to church on the Lord's Day and attended an English Bible class which was taught by a foreigner. In those days there was a famous Chinese preacher by the name of Chiao Weichen, who in 1935 organised the first Manchurian Christian conference at the Yingkou Bible Institute.

The main speaker was to be the Peking independent pastor, Rev. Wang Ming Tao. Professor Chiao obtained a special half-price ticket discount from the South Manchuria Railway Company for all who wished to attend this conference. It was a great attraction to me, and to satisfy my curiosity I registered to attend the conference, partly because I wished to see the ocean and the big ocean liners. Unbeknown to me God was to use this conference as an opportunity to work in my heart.

Mr. Wang Ming Tao preached in the power of

the Holy Spirit. The second evening of the conference, as I prayed before going to bed, the Holy Spirit mightily illuminated my heart. The sins which I had committed in the past now flashed across my mind as on a cinema screen. Under the conviction of the Holy Spirit, I confessed these sins one by one before God, and asked the Lord to cleanse me with the precious blood of his Son, Jesus Christ.

On the third day, there was such a hunger and thirst in my heart that I felt like a baby craving the pure milk of the Word. When I left the conference for home on the train the mountains and trees on both sides of the railroad seemed to me to be brand new. My heart was filled with such joy and happiness that even nature was transformed. On my return, the family, too, recognised that I had been changed. I read the Psalms every day, and I had a deep wish to dedicate myself to serve God all the days of my life.

Peichen High School was operated by the Yingkou Church. Prior to the conclusion of the Yingkou Conference, the Principal extended an invitation to Christian parents to send their children there. Since I had made the decision to dedicate myself to the service of God, Peichen High School seemed to me to be an ideal place to secure preparatory education for pursuing theological education in the future. I wrote to the Principal telling him of my hopes, and was accepted soon afterwards as a student. In September 1936, at the age of twenty, I graduated and entered Yingkou Bible Institute.

The same year my first son, Theodore, was born.

## 5

*Do not forsake your mother when she is old*
*(Proverbs 23:22)*

It was at this period that my mother became blind. She had always enjoyed good vision and was able to do needlework even when she was over sixty.

In 1937, financial circumstances decreed that my mother and my wife and family would have to rent accommodation while I continued at the Institute. They stayed with a family called Liu who were Buddhists.

One day the Lius wanted to have an idol-worshipping ceremony at which outsiders were not allowed to be present. My mother and wife were asked to spend the night elsewhere. My wife took the children to our cousin's home, while my mother, due to her old age, stayed with a relative of the Liu family nearby. She had trouble going to sleep that night, so she rose and started to do some knitting. But a sudden headache struck her. Her sleep was ruined, and she could not rest at all.

The following day Mr. Liu came to my wife.

'Your old mother did not sleep well last night,' he said. They gave her an acupuncture treatment as had been done with previous headaches and she felt better. The next morning, while my mother was still in bed, she said to my wife, 'What time is it? Why is it not dawn yet?'

As my wife replied, 'It's already eight o'clock in the morning,' she lit a match and waved it to and fro before my mother's eyes. There was no reaction. She realised that my mother had become blind.

When I received this news I hurried back home from Yingkou and took my mother to the Christian hospital. After examination, the doctor said to her, 'Madam, we are both Christians, so you know that I will not lie to you. There is no hope for your eyes. But look at it this way - you have already seen all the things in the world. Now you can enjoy more quietness of mind when you do not have to look at this world, and you can concentrate on unseen realities. You can pray more constantly for your son and for the church.'

'My heart is now at peace,' said my mother. 'I don't have to go here and there trying to look for a cure.'

There was never one moment of sadness in her attitude after that. She continued to do her household chores in an orderly way, humming

Christian hymns as she worked, right to the day of her death in 1944 at the age of seventy-five.

Looking back at her life I am deeply conscious of the many hardships which she had to endure. Our family was far from perfect, but God in his mercy visited her in her forty-seventh year and gave her a son in her old age. She left this world in peace, charging me just before she breathed her last breath to be a good preacher. I rejoice that she was able to lead at least one of her six children to know and serve the Lord.

There is a Chinese proverb which says, 'The tree wants to be still, but the wind keeps on blowing; the son wishes to wait on his parents, but they are no longer there.' This proverb vividly expresses my own feelings. I still long to serve my mother and to greet her in the morning and the evening of each day.

# 6

*These men are the servants of the most high God*
*(Acts 16:17)*

The old Christian theological seminary in Mukden had unfortunately come under the control of the liberal church. Most of its graduates were sceptical about important Biblical doctrines such as the inspiration of the Scriptures, the miracles, the virgin birth of Jesus, and his resurrection. This was a great tragedy for the preaching of the gospel, and many Christians worried about the future of the church.

It was for this reason that the Rev. James McCommon, a missionary of the Presbyterian Church of Ireland, founded the Yingkou Bible Institute in 1930. His bold step under the guidance of the Holy Spirit was not without hardships and opposition, but he established it for the training of Chinese preachers in the orthodox faith.

Young Christian men and women who were called by God to serve him flocked to this Bible Institute from all parts of Manchuria. Its opening made big news, for people recognised that it belonged to the fundamentalists. Later, when Mr. McCommon had raised enough money in England, a new four-storey building was built in 1935 with capacity for more than a hundred students. When I entered Yingkou Bible Institute in 1936, the student enrolment was at its peak. In our class alone there were thirty-two students from different churches in Manchuria.

At that time the Institute was under dispensational leadership. My favourite textbook then was the Scofield Reference Bible. Not many people knew anything about Scofield, the man or his theological views, but we liked his Bible on account of all his footnotes. Actually, the Scofield Bible is the standard textbook of the Dispensational school of interpretation.

After an internship in North Manchuria, I returned to Yingkou Bible Institute for further study in 1938 to discover that a new professor had come to teach. This was the American missionary, Johannes G. Vos, on loan to Yingkou Bible Institute from the American Reformed Presbyterian Mission of Tsitsihar, Manchuria. Rev Vos became my best teacher and friend, and from that time on contributed greatly to my understanding of the Bible.

Rev. McCommon had once spent a Sabbatical

year at Princeton Theological Seminary in America where Rev. Vos' famous father, Dr. Geerhardus Vos, was professor of Biblical Theology. There he came to know Dr. Vos the professor, as well as his son, Johannes Vos. After Mr. McCommon found out that the younger Vos was working in the Reformed Presbyterian Mission at Tsitsihar in North Manchuria, he was able by various diplomatic manoeuvrings to persuade him to come to Yingkou Bible Institute to teach.

Rev. Vos was our systematic theology teacher during my final year at the Institute. At the time, I was under the influence of the prevailing Dispensationalism taught in the Yingkou school. Under Rev. Vos' instruction my thinking underwent a great change. For example, my former conviction had been that regeneration always comes after faith. Mr. Vos taught us that regeneration comes first, and faith follows. He was teaching us the Reformed or Calvinistic system of theology. We often debated this and other points of theology in our systematic theology class, as well as in private conversations with this new teacher.

I was also attracted by Rev. Vos' love and humility as a man. After class, I often went to his home and had long conversations with him, usually concerning the differences between Dispensationalism and the Reformed Faith. He would cite passages from Scripture and theological classics to make his point, and he showed unlimited patience as he answered my questions. In this manner a profound friendship grew up between us.

\* \* \* \* \* \*

In June of 1938 Yingkou Bible Institute held its eighth beginning-of-term ceremony. The special guest speaker on that occasion was the Rev. Charles Leonard, a missionary from the American Baptist Church mission. He had worked first in the Shantung province so he spoke Chinese with a heavy Shantung accent. His forty minute address was punctuated with so much humour and his accent was so funny that we laughed all the time.

He encouraged us, saying, 'Whenever you encounter problems as you go out to preach do not even say, "It's impossible!" ' He opened up his jacket and showed us his belt buckle, and said, 'Look at this belt buckle. This was a gift which our school gave to every graduate at commencement time. The Latin words inscribed on it mean: *Do not ever say, There is no way out. When there seems to be no plan, think of a plan. If you can't think of any plan, make a plan!'*

After graduation I was invited to work with Rev. Leonard in Harbin. Soon I was reassigned to pioneer evangelism in Chingkang County and for the very first time in my life I set foot on the Great Northern Wilderness.

Here the scenery was desolate and the food strange to my taste. It was approaching winter and the weather was turning very cold. Nevertheless it was most challenging to do evangelistic work in the country. People came to the town to shop in the open air market on certain days of the week, so we used those market days to hold evangelistic meetings in the church. Many people attended.

Our meals were served in the dining-room of the deacon's home. Here I met a high school classmate who had come to a meeting and both of us felt especially close to each other under such circumstances. After that he often came to the church to worship God and to study the Bible.

## 7

*Guide me in your truth and teach me*
(Psalm 25:5)

Like lightning out of a clear sky, a notice came to Yingkou Bible Institute from the Manchurian Government telling them that all religious schools which had not registered with the government must close. Rev. McCommon was British, and since relations between Great Britain and Japan were not good at the time, the school was forced to close. He turned his school over to six American citizens and returned to Ireland.

One of those six was J.G. Vos and he was elected president. One day when I was preaching in Chingkang, I received a letter from Rev. Vos in which he told me of the recent closing of the school and of his plan to reopen it. He earnestly urged me to return to be his assistant. So at the end of the year I resigned my post at Peitahuang and at the beginning of 1940 I moved my whole family - mother, wife and children - back to Yingkou Bible Institute and began work with Rev. Vos.

Since the school had been closed by the order of the Manchurian Government, everything had to be started all over again. In accordance with our plan, the president of the school first wrote letters to the local Military Police headquarters, the local civilian police department, the American Consul-General in Mukden, and the Education Ministry at Changchun, to report that the Yingkou Bible Institute was to reopen in September. After formal notice had been given to all, the school was officially reopened in September.

After the reopening of our school, secret police from the Government often interrogated me concerning every imaginable thing. This was a real headache to me.

My work was to translate Rev. Vos' lecture notes into Chinese for the students. It was while I was working with Rev. Vos that he gave me the book *The Reformed Doctrine of Predestination*, by Dr. Loraine Boettner. Mr. Vos introduced it to me in these words: 'During my days at Princeton Theological Seminary the author of this book, Dr. Boettner, was a fellow-student of mine. He was a quiet fellow and I never imagined that he would ever write such a big book as this. I sincerely recommend that you read it for I am sure that it will be a great help to your faith.'

Then I began to read the English volume. The

purpose of this book is to explain the truth of the Bible concerning God's predestination of all things. Dr. Boettner does an excellent job in expounding that doctrine. He quotes from many sources to explain it, analysing every detail. After I had read the book I truly felt that I had received much help from it. I wrote a letter to the author and told him that I was a colleague of Rev. J.G. Vos, and that I had a burden to translate his book into Chinese to help Chinese believers to understand the profound doctrine of predestination.

Dr. Boettner replied immediately. He sent me another copy of the latest edition of his book and with it a few copies of another book which he had written, *The Inspiration of the Scriptures*. He told me frankly that I ought to begin by translating this book because the inspiration of Scripture is the foundation of all other doctrines. After that, I was much interested in all the books which Dr. Boettner wrote and tried to study each of them in depth.

Only six months from the time Yingkou Bible Institute was reopened another order came from the Education Department of the Manchurian Government. This order stated that the government did not recognise any school operated by the church. Soon agents from the Military Police came to our school to enforce the order and demanded that we close as soon as possible. The new students sadly prepared to return to their homes.

Mr. Vos and I discussed at length what to do. We drew up a provisional one-year plan. He asked me to be caretaker of the school in hope that it could be reopened as soon as circumstances would permit. On March 5th, 1941, Rev. Vos left the Manchurian church which he had served for more than ten years and returned to the United States, where he became the pastor of a small rural church in Kansas. It was during my caretakership that I translated into Chinese Dr. Boettner's *Inspiration of the Scriptures.*

On December 8th that year Japan suddenly attacked Pearl Harbor and the Pacific War began. Conditions in Manchuria immediately became tense. All those Chinese who had former connections with Britain or America feared arrest and imprisonment. Next door to our school was a large building which housed the foreign Chamber of Commerce. As I watched it being occupied by Japanese soldiers, I said to my wife, 'Prepare some padded trousers for me' (to be worn in prison if they arrested me). But, thank God, the Japanese took no action against the caretaker of Yingkou Bible Institute.

In the summer of 1942, a certain Japanese pastor named Rev. Ishikawa Shiro came to take over our school under the authority of the Committee to Confiscate Church properties in Manchuria. I turned over all the property of the school to Mr. Ishikawa, so concluding my job of caretaker which had began fourteen months before.

## 8

*The Lord will keep you from all evil*
*(Psalm 121:7)*

Tashihchiao - 'Great Stone Bridge' - was an important city in Southern Manchuria. The church there belonged to the Presbyterian Church of Ireland.

Old Pastor Kao was at first very zealous when he became a believer. But he had been arrested by Japanese military police and put in prison during the 1931 invasion of Manchuria. This experience and the lingering fears of a similar danger made him extremely reluctant to deal with matters outside the church. He was approaching retirement age anyway, so the church was eager to find a young assistant for him.

My former teacher and the dean of Yingkou Bible Institute, the Rev. Yang Chingtsun, became pastor of the Western Church at Yingkou when our Institute was first ordered to be closed. At this moment the Tashihchiao church requested Rev. Yang to help them find a younger man as associate pastor. The reason was that Japanese special agents often came to the church and troubled the old pastor, investigating the church's political thinking and so on. If the church had a younger man to take care of these agents and other problems, it would be more satisfactory. Rev. Yang asked me to accept the position.

I served as associate pastor of the Tashihchiao Presbyterian Church from October 1942 to August 1945, the year Japan surrendered. The old pastor and I took turns filling the pulpit each week. He seldom read his Bible, relying rather on recounting his own experiences, so he would babble a lot in the pulpit, sometimes saying nothing beyond telling trivial stories about his own household. When you visited the pastor's home, you would see piles of Chinese novels stacked under the tea table, books such as 'Romance of the Three Kingdoms', 'Chronicles of the Eastern Chou Dynasty', 'Story of the Seven Knights' and 'Heroes of the Water Marsh'.

The old pastor had already reached the age of retirement, and his church had purchased a house, with an orchard, for him to live in after he retired. But now that a younger associate pastor had been employed to take care of outside affairs with the public, the pastor had even less to do than before, so he was more reluctant to retire than ever!

There were two elders at Tashihchiao - Wu and Kuo. Both of them were rich men who had started out with nothing but empty hands.

Elder Wu had once dedicated himself to be a preacher when he was young, and had even studied theology for a few days! But then he made a lot of money from business and became one of the richest men in Southern Manchuria. He felt somewhat guilty for going back on his youthful vow to be a minister, so he was particularly zealous in the work of the church, as a means of restitution.

Like Elder Wu, Elder Kuo was very successful in business. Each man founded a church in his home town, hiring the preachers and paying all their expenses. Thus they became in control of the church.

The church at Tashihchiao could seat three hundred people; yet they never took up an offering during the services. These two rich elders said, 'If we collect offerings, the non-Christians will say that we are here to make money.' To cover church expenses, the congregation made a general contribution each year at Christmas time. The deacons would open a big book and ask people to sign up for contributions. Then they would post the names of the contributors on the wall of the church office. Afterwards, the elders and deacons would assemble to discuss the next year's budget. If a deficit occurred, the rich elders would make up most of the difference. In this way, the impression was given to the church members that they would have no financial problems in the church as long as the two elders were there.

At the same time, the pastor was extremely respectful and subservient to these two. He would walk out to the front gate to welcome them whenever they came to church, and go out with them to see them off as they left. My heart was filled with sadness as I watched this pitiful performance by the pastor: he was not unlike a pet dog wagging its tail at the master.

Then there was the question of my salary. Though the church was well off financially it did not treat its preacher as it should have done. They treated the younger preacher like a hireling, whose salary must not equal that of the old pastor. Under the Manchukuo Government then in power all food was rationed. With a wife, mother and my four children to feed, the support of my family became a heavy burden. Life for us was so miserable in those days that my wife vowed that she would never wish any of her sons to become preachers!

The Japanese military authorities wanted all religious organisations to appoint representatives to attend air defence seminars and drills, so that they could go back to their congregations and train the church members in civil air-raid defence manoeuvres. This job naturally fell to me as part of the church's official dealings with outside agencies. Still no word was spoken about adjusting my salary to our living expenses.

One day, Elder Kuo was having a wedding for his grandson. Both the pastor and I were invited. The older man officiated and I was master of ceremonies. When the wedding ceremony was over and the feast began, Pastor Kao was asked to sit at the table of honour while I was asked to sit with other guests at a side table.

Being young and impulsive at that time, I thought they were deliberately insulting me. Of course Kao was older and he was the senior pastor of the church. But wasn't I an associate pastor of the same church? Why did they invite him to sit at the head table and not me? Infuriated by this insult, I rose and walked out of the place.

Elder Kuo sent a woman preacher after me to ask me to return, lest we should be embarrassed to meet one another in the future. I did return and Elder Kuo scolded me for my imprudence. Some years later, after I moved to Hong Kong and published the first issues of our magazine *Faith and Life,* I sent a copy to Elder Kuo. In his reply he wrote, 'I never expected to hear such good reports from you in my life time' (1 Timothy 3:2-5).

* * * * * *

One day in 1944 a man from the Japanese Military Police Department came to see me at my home.

'Did you formerly stay in Yingkou?' he asked.

'Yes.'

'Did you work with the Americans?'

'Yes.'

'Did the Americans leave you a telegraph transmitter and tell you to send telegrams to them?'

'Oh, no.'

After more questioning, he told me to report at the Military Police Department at nine o'clock the next morning. In those days the people thought of going to the Military Police Department as the worst possible activity, for most people who went there never returned. I had no appetite that evening. I really did not know what to do and felt absolutely helpless.

After breakfast the following morning I said to my wife, 'The chances are pretty high that I will never return from the Department. If that does happen I hope that you will take good care of the children and my mother. See to it that she dies in peace.' My wife burst into tears as she saw me off.

On the way to the Department I went to visit my good friend, Wong Changpu, who ran a clock and watch store in the town.

'Mr. Chao,' he said, 'why are you here so early?'

I took him aside and told him the whole story.

'You preachers are too naive,' he said. 'These Military Police are the worst kind of people. Never mind them, and don't go to the Military Police Department either. You just go home and let me take care of it.'

So I took his advice, returned to my home and told my wife what had happened.

'I was praying the whole time since you left,' she said, 'I asked the Lord to bring you back in peace so that you could serve him and take care of your family. Let us continue to commit this whole matter to the Lord.'

I learned afterwards that the Japanese official was only trying to get me to pay him bribe money. Mr. Wong went to see him that day, took him out to dinner, wined him and dined him and the whole problem disappeared. Thank God it was a false alarm!

\* \* \* \* \* \*

Our fourth son, Harry, was born on February 9th, 1945. Shortly after the Dragon Boat Festival that year, our third son, Samuel, suddenly became sick with a fever. He would neither eat nor drink. My wife took him to a doctor but he could not find out the cause of the illness. The boy wanted my wife to hold him in her arms all day long and did not even want her to nurse the baby, Harry. Fortunately, our second son, Jonathan, was old enough to take care of Harry, which was a great help to his mother.

Sam's condition became worse and worse. His body was reduced to mere skin and bones, and his voice sounded as weak as a kitten's. Fearing that the child might die, my wife wrote a letter to me in Mukden and asked me to come home as soon as possible. When I saw Samuel, we discussed the problem and prayed that in case God was going to take him home, we would have the boy baptised. But if the Lord was not going to take him, we would pray that the Lord would heal his sickness, and if he recovered we would dedicate Samuel to the service of God.

We asked the Rev. Lee Tienching to come and baptise Samuel. That same evening Sam suddenly said he was thirsty. We were overjoyed. Ever since he became ill he had not asked for food or drink! The next day my wife made porridge for him, and he finished a whole bowl of it. Gradually, from that time, he recovered fully from his sickness. As he grew up, we did not forget our vows and we also reminded Sam that he belonged to God.

When Sam grew to manhood, he offered himself to God. After graduating from college he went to a seminary to study theology. He went to Taiwan in 1977 and served as chaplain at Chung-yuan Christian University. By God's grace, he met

Miss Yueh-na Chung there and later married her. They returned to the United States to work in an American church in 1980. ✓

## 9

*Though an army besiege me, my heart will not fear*
*(Psalm 27:3)*

It was the 15th of August, 1945. Over the radio we heard that the Emperor of Japan had surrendered and that war in the Pacific was now over. All who heard it were so elated that they were almost crazy with joy! Still, it was better not to make too much noise about it: there were still Japanese patrols all around. But in just two days the market changed from inactivity to great prosperity and all kinds of roadside stands retailing popular food items began to reappear. Even the underground Chinese communists came out of hiding.

A few days later, however, the Russian troops poured in like a flood. They came in from the north to the south by railroads, highways and trucks. All order broke down after they entered a city: they bought things and gave no money; they ate things without paying the merchants; they robbed the Japanese military warehouses and sold what they had stolen to the Chinese people, in exchange for used wrist watches and old fountain pens. I saw with my own eyes a Chinese trade a watch to a Russian for more than ten Japanese military blankets which the soldier had stolen. Wherever the Russian soldiers went the Chinese children would give the 'thumbs up' sign and shout 'Shang kao!' - 'Number 1!' and the Soviet soldiers would shout back, 'Shang Kao!'

The railway system broke down: railway stations were in a mess, some people even making their homes in them. Goods shipments stopped completely. Only one passenger train southward and one northward were allowed to move each day. The Russians tore down all heavy industry plants and shipped the equipment northward. They robbed farmers of their cattle and shipped them to Darien. Politically, economically and socially, Manchuria now entered a stage of total confusion.

Chinese civilians had a rough time. All families kept their houses tightly locked at all times and women especially were afraid of suffering violence by Russian soldiers.

I remember the first time I was bothered by them. Mrs. Kao, a woman evangelist from our church, was knocking on our door. At that point three Russian soldiers appeared and yelled in

Russian, 'Woman! Woman!' Mrs. Kao was terrified. I opened the door quickly and Mrs. Kao rushed inside. The soldiers approached. 'Are there women here?'

I answered with the only Russian words I knew. 'This is a church. There is no woman here. Please go away.' I later learned that what I had actually said was 'Let's go away'.

They started to leave, but as I was about to shut the door one of them turned and kicked it open while another pointed his pistol at my head. The third grabbed me by the arm and dragged me along the street.

'Oh Lord,' I prayed as I walked, 'please deliver me out of the hands of these evil men.'

They wanted me to find women for them. But how or where could I do that? People said that if you did find girls for these soldiers they would give you some reward, but if you didn't they would shoot you dead on the spot.

I was reaching the end of my wits when a tenwheeler truck came speeding along from the north and stopped right in front of us. There was an exchange in Russian between the men on board and the three with me. Two of my captors jumped on to the truck; the third patted me on the shoulder and made hand signs. 'Alasho!' - 'You may go!' As the truck sped away I thanked God for hearing my prayer. I ran back to the church at full speed, found the gate closed, and climbed over the wall at the back. My family had been praying for me. When my wife saw me return safe, she gave glory to our Father in heaven.

After the arrival of the Russians, there emerged underground agents of the KMT - Kuomintang - Chiang Kai-Shek's Nationalist Government. Having learned that I worked for the church and also understood a little English, they thought that I might possibly be of some help to them.

One day an unexpected guest came to our church. I had no idea who he was. He was dressed quite oddly and looked like a typical farmer from the country. 'Don't you know me?' he said. 'I am Chen.'

Then I remembered him, my friend Chen. He had worked at a Manchurian bank and was a very humble, gentle man. He had often come to visit me in Yingkou. We were both young and got along well. He spoke good Japanese but he also wanted to learn English from me. Later he was arrested by the Japanese on a charge of being a Kuomintang spy, but when the Russians entered Manchuria after the Japanese surrender, they released all prisoners who had been arrested as underground agents for the KMT. Most of these were in Yingkou.

'We really need people like you to help us,' he said.

'Certainly,' I replied. 'We are all Chinese and I love the Central Government. I will do whatever I can.' Two days later he sent us a big bag of rice.

He was a key figure in KMT's underground. Because of his arrest and sufferings in prison he was now in charge of KMT co-ordination work between Yingkou and Tashihchiao. Since I worked for the church and understood English they saw that I could possibly help them and so I was invited to join in their discussions - even if it was only to think up welcome slogans for the American troops!

Communist secret agents also surfaced at this time, and there was great confusion before the Central Government of China came in to take control. Communists captured and killed KMT agents; KMT agents captured and killed Communist agents.

Soviet Russia did not miss this opportunity to 'fish in troubled waters' either. Superficially, they professed to be helping the KMT but secretly they gave many supplies to the Chinese Communists. So there were gains and losses on both sides. Whenever the KMT lost ground, the Communist agents would emerge and make trouble all over the place.

For a short time the Communists investigated

people to find willing collaborators with the Government. At one group of villages where I went to evangelise, the Communist agents worked through the local post office where the postmaster was himself an agent. He placed my name on their list as one who had contacts with the KMT.

\* \* \* \* \* \*

It was during those days of Communist activity that news came from Tiehling that my wife's mother was seriously ill; she wanted her daughter to hurry home. We failed to get on board the daily northbound train at our first attempt with our few belongings and six children, and had to go back home and risk being visited again by the Communists by night.

The following day, the train was just as full. Deacon Wong had come to see me off. 'Mr. Chao, how can you get on that train?'

I braced myself. 'Oh God!' I cried, 'I must get on this train today.'

I pounded with my fist on a closed coach window. An old man inside gestured as if to say, 'You'll never find room in here'. I continued to implore his help and he reluctantly opened the window. I was still young and fit enough to crawl in quite easily; all six children were handed up to me one by one; finally, my wife was pushed through, dressed in men's clothing and with her face painted to give the appearance of an ordinary worker. The disguise was essential if we were to negotiate safely a point on the line where, it was said, Russian soldiers always boarded, ostensibly to look for 'explosives' but actually to look for women.

At Pingtingpao eight hours later, we left the train as we had boarded it - through the window! It was a rush; there was not even time to count the children. Suddenly, Jonathan said, 'Look, Daddy, there's someone lying on the rails under the train!' It was our second daughter, Jean! She was wearing a red coat and so was easily seen. I reached down and dragged her up just as the train began to move. How sincerely I thanked God!

It was three miles from the station to the Lee home, three miles through snow and past Communist checkpoints. When my mother-in-law saw her daughter, her courage returned. She left her bed and chatted and laughed heartily. But the joyful reunion was only the glow before the sunset. She died a few days later at the age of fifty-four.

She was a sincere, humble, diligent woman who had managed her household well. Sadly, however, she had never believed in the Lord Jesus.

My wife's family were considered well-to-do. Mr. Lee and a brother ran a blacksmith's business. Because of railway traffic problems at the time, there arose a greater demand for horse-drawn carts and so my father-in-law was kept busy. I worked with him as a bill-collector, running round among customers with my lantern until late at night.

\* \* \* \* \* \*

As time went on, Communist activity increased. People looked to the day when the Central Government would take control. Meanwhile, Central Government and Russia negotiated. Nationalists were forbidden to enter Manchuria which remained largely under Russian control, and Russia intentionally delayed military withdrawal until Chinese Communists could gain a foothold. Finally, with the assistance of the United States Fleet, Central Government forces arrived and our hope of many years was realised - Manchuria, it seemed, had returned to the bosom of her motherland, China.

There was great excitement as the New First Army entered our city with American jeeps, guns and tanks. Peace and tranquillity had finally come to stay in Manchuria. Things which had been lying in desolation were to be renewed. We began to resume normal living. A bright future seemed to be on the way.

But, as the saying goes, good times never last.

As the Russian army departed, it handed all its equipment and supplies to the Communist Chinese in northern Manchuria. The Nationalists busily repaired road and rail communications and moved into major cities in the south. The Communists, meantime, gathered strength and civil war finally broke out between the Communist North and the Nationalist South of Manchuria. Life became even more difficult: the see-saw nature of the conflict meant that we had to move with the Nationalists as they gained ground or lost it. This tense way of life continued through 1946 and 1947.

I had returned to Mukden without my family in the winter of 1946. It was during this period that I found myself working as a slave-labourer. One Lord's Day, in the winter of 1946, I had set out to go to church. Heavy snow was falling, so I changed my plan and took a short-cut through an alley to a nearby chapel. As I emerged from the alley, a Russian soldier walked up to me, pointing a gun, and clearly indicated that I should follow him. We entered what turned out to be an ice factory. More than thirty Chinese were standing there.

'Why have they brought us here?' I asked the man beside me. 'Who knows?' he replied.

As thirty or so more Chinese came up from the basement, we were ordered down. Our job was to clean up the basement, arrange the piles of ice blocks, pick up the garbage and throw it out - including a dead dog which we dug up. The job took three hours. I never got to church that day. Although some of the older Chinese knew a little Russian and tried it out on the soldiers, 'Officer, have you had your dinner? Let's go, OK,' the only answer they ever got was 'Dawei!' 'Work!'

After this I moved with my family to Chungku. Our son William was born there in August 1947. At the time, the Communist military control had reached its peak and the Nationalists retreated to the larger cities; they gave up the railway station near our home and the Communists set fire to it. It was frightening to watch the smoke of the burning building rising into the sky.

The time of the baby's delivery arrived but the electricity had been cut off and we could not find a midwife. In desperation, I had to take over myself! With no medical training and no experience, I cut the umbilical cord - too far from the baby's body, as it happened, and although there was some infection later, everything turned out all right. We thanked God for his great grace and named the little boy, Wei-en - 'Great Grace'.

Early one morning a few days later, two local Communist party members arrived at our home with guns in their hands. I was forced into a shop at the other side of the street. A crowd was already there. This, it transpired, was the headquarters of the local Communists and they were gathering a Commando force to help in an attack on the Nationalist-held-bridge to the south. We would act as a living shield, marching at gun-point in front of the Communists.

As their leader began speaking, a phone rang and he went to answer it. An old man beside me in the back row immediately saw a chance to slip away. I followed him and hid with him in a nearby pig-shed. Although he was not too pleased that I should follow him, we were both safe for the moment; in the crisis I had benefited from the older man's age and wisdom.

After this escape my wife and I decided that I should leave as it was becoming dangerous for me to continue living in Chungku. I went first to my father-in-law's home but I realised while there that I would be safer in Mukden. But even there life was difficult.

One day I noticed a newspaper advertisement in which the United Nations Relief and Rehabilitation Administration - UNRRA - were asking for Chinese translators. I applied, took the examination and was accepted.

My work was to receive American relief supplies at Mukden and to transport them north - tractors, reaping machines, cars, jeeps, medicines, medical instruments, blankets, DDT - always accompanied by armed guards. Security was critical. We could only relax when freight trucks were finally loaded and we were on the move.

But I grew tired of secular work. Although I had been compelled by family economic circumstances to take a job 'in the world' and indeed gained much valuable experience, I was after all, a preacher of the gospel. I felt out of place.

One application for supplies came from the Chungcheng Middle School in my home town of Kaiyuan. There I met the headmaster who readily agreed that I might teach English in his school in the future. A few months later, Kaiyuan was besieged by the Communists and the school moved south to Mukden; here I had my chance to teach for a short time.

Then I moved to the YMCA at Mukden where apart from teaching English I had opportunities to witness to Chinese refugees and I was blessed with some fruit from those contacts in 1947. Thirty years later my son Samuel, serving as chaplain in a Christian College in Taiwan, discovered that Mr. Lee, the president of the College, had studied English with me in the YMCA at Mukden. I had forgotten all about it and so I was delighted when the chance came to meet Mr. Lee himself once again.

During my time of residence at the YMCA, I had frequent correspondence with my American friends: Rev. Vos recommended me for study in Faith Seminary in the United States; Dr. Boettner pledged financial help with my travel expenses. In time a telegram arrived from the Seminary announcing that I had been accepted and that all expenses would be taken care of. There was no trouble getting a visa from the United States Consulate; all I needed now was a Chinese passport from Nanking, there being no office in Manchuria. I would go there by way of Shanghai.

Then came the great trial of my faith. How could I leave my wife and seven children in a Manchuria torn by disorder and fraught with danger? Where could I safely leave them? It was impossible to get as large a family as that out of the country.

But it was at this point of crisis that miracles began to happen.

## 10

*The rough ways shall be made smooth*
*(Luke 3:18)*

It was my custom to have my devotions every morning in my YMCA office. On one such morning in the spring of 1948 - a Saturday - three foreigners arrived.

One introduced himself as Mr. Olson of the Lutheran Church. They had come to Mukden, he said, to airlift five hundred Koreans and their dependants to Peking. When their week's contract was completed, they would be flying to Shanghai.

'Do you know a Mr. Greene at the China Seminary there?' he asked. 'He is holding some money for your travel to the United States.'

'Yes,' I said, 'I had often corresponded with Mr. Greene.'

Mr. Olson announced that he was going to take me to Shanghai. I was amazed and overjoyed. It was practically impossible to get on a plane at Mukden at the time because all commercial planes were monopolised by the authorities. And the

American consulate plane with its fourteen seats was fully booked for five months or more. Now here was a stranger telling me I could hop aboard his plane immediately! Surely my first step in my life-long dream of studying abroad! My joy knew no bounds.

But my dilemma concerning my family had to be revealed to Mr. Olson. He was sympathetic but he could not help: he had to return to Shanghai in five days.

On the Monday, I established through my wife's relatives in Tiehling that I could not possibly return to my family because of Communist activity. On the Tuesday, in Mukden, I made up my own mind and packed my belongings. On the Thursday, I boarded Mr. Olson's plane for Shanghai. The flight took two days, stopping overnight at Peking. I took the opportunity of visiting my spiritual father, Wang Ming Tao, with whom I enjoyed an evening of fellowship.

It had been the Rev. Albert Greene to whom Dr. Boettner had entrusted the travel money and who had organised my flight on the 'mercy plane'. When he learned of my financial needs, he gave me a temporary job translating articles on archaeology into Chinese. I had frequent opportunities for fellowship with him: we talked about our families; he was surprised to hear I had seven children, having assumed that I was unmarried.

'What, then, are you going to do with your family?' he asked.

I told him of my tentative plan to get a passport at Nanking and go to the States.

He was clearly troubled. 'As a Christian,' he said, 'I think that what you are doing is wrong.' He quoted 1 Timothy 5:8: 'If anyone does not provide for his relatives, and especially for his immediate family, he has denied the faith and is worse than an unbeliever.'

There was a real struggle in my heart. I knew Mr. Greene was right. If I left China for the United States under the present circumstances I would have no peace.

'We must pray,' said Mr. Greene, 'that God would bring your family out of the dangerous area where they are now. That is your most urgent problem.

So we prayed, and I decided to stay at the Seminary until the Lord told me what to do. His intervention came one day in April.

'I have good news for you, Brother Chao,' said Mr. Greene. 'The Lutheran 'mercy' plane is going to Manchuria again and will be returning to Shanghai.'

He had already told the Lutheran Centre about my problem and they had agreed that my family should be airlifted provided that air fares could be guaranteed and that my family could get to Mukden to be picked up in seven days. This last proviso was a problem: it was a long distance from my family's village to Mukden. Nevertheless, I gave the 'mercy' plane pilots the names of my family along with a letter to be mailed to my wife from Mukden, telling her to get there as soon as possible. I then committed the whole matter to God in earnest prayer.

As the week went by, I was in constant telephone contact with Mr. Nelson of the Lutheran Mission Centre. On the evening of the day my family was to have boarded the plane, he phoned to say that the aircraft had developed mechanical problems and would be delayed for two days. I breathed a sigh of relief! My family would now have ample time to reach Mukden! I knelt and gave thanks to God with a heart full of praise. Now I knew for sure that he would bring my family to Shanghai.

A day or so later I phoned Mr. Nelson. 'Good news!' he said. 'The plane will arrive this afternoon.'

Just after noon, I arrived at Lunghua Airport. I did not have long to wait. There it came - a silver plane with the flag of the Republic of China painted on its sides and the name *St Paul* under it. Gracefully, it touched down and taxied up the runway, closer and closer. My heart beat violently!

Then the plane came to a complete stop. The door opened. First out was my wife with our baby son, Bill, in her arms. I was too moved to speak. I silently thanked God from the depths of a happy heart.

## 11

*A virtuous woman is a crown to her husband.*
*(Proverbs 12:4)*

**Mrs. Chao's account of her escape to Shanghai.**

On the same night that our son, Bill, was born, August 21st, 1947, the Chinese Communist army entered Chungku. Shortly after that, because his life was in danger, I urged my husband to flee first to my parents' home from where he went to Mukden. From then until we were reunited at Shanghai Airport in May 1948, our family suffered separation, anxiety, and all the daily inconveniences and perils of life in the middle of a civil war between the Communists and the Nationalists.

\* \* \* \* \* \*

After Charles was forced to go and I had to cope with seven children in our house in Chungku, tears were never far from my eyes. Communist soldiers occupied the town. They confiscated food from all the homes, and took what I had in the house. But they did not find the ten sacks of grain we had hidden to be bartered for money if we ever had to leave.

Only two days after my husband left we had nothing in the house to eat. Relatives tried to comfort me. One of these was a sister-in-law of my husband. My baby had been crying for an hour when she came in and exclaimed, 'What smells so bad here?'

'There were no lights when I gave birth to my baby,' I said. 'Maybe we did not clean up the place well. My husband tried his best to clean up things before he left.'

My sister-in-law unwrapped the swaddling clothes around the baby. 'Ah, so this is where the smell is coming from,' she said. 'It seems that nobody treated the severed umbilical cord at all! Look the baby's navel is just rotting!'

I sent Ted to the midwife immediately and when she inspected the baby, she exclaimed, 'The child's bowels are visible through the navel! I don't think he is going to make it!'

My husband had been my only helper at the delivery of the baby. He had boiled water and had washed the baby clean. But nobody had put disinfectant on the cut umbilical cord! The midwife did the best she could, and after we wrapped him up and gave him some milk, the baby stopped crying. Only then did my heart begin to have peace, and I finally got some rest. Thankfully, the baby recovered.

* * * * * *

Every evening there was a curfew. After dark nobody knew when bullets would begin to fly or where they might strike. One night, after I had put the children to bed and was preparing to go to bed myself, some Communists came knocking at our door. Earlier that day I had hung a sign on the door - Maternity Ward - because I had heard that Communists would not enter a maternity ward in case of contamination. But in the dark they could not see my sign. I told them about it, but they would not believe me and I had to open the door before they would accept that it really was a maternity room. They left without entering.

I dared not undress now and go to bed. Nobody knew when another band of Communists might come, and if they came I would have to open my door again. Although the first group had told me to leave my door open, I did not dare do so in case somebody would come in and rob me. The rest of the night I sat on the edge of the bed in my quilted jacket. By dawn I was totally exhausted. The children lost sleep too because of the frequent knockings at our door. Things were much better during the day when the soldiers could read the sign.

Two days after my husband left, we were out of food. The crops were ready in our area, but nobody was in the mood for harvesting as long as the Communists were all around. So the crops were left in the field to rot. Ten-year-old Ted and eight year old Jonathan went to the fields to pick green soy beans. These were cooked and eaten with only water to drink and that was how the children lived through those days. It was even worse for me, a nursing mother, with very little else to eat. I cooked some rice gruel for myself from the rice that I had previously hidden and this was supplemented by some millet given to me by a cousin's wife who saw how pale I looked.

Five days after my husband's departure, the Nationalists counter-attacked and the Communists retreated. Some Nationalist soldiers stayed in part of our house and because there were officers among them, guards were stationed at our door every night.

So I was no longer afraid to take out more of the food which I had hidden and cook it for my children. Ted ground some flour and I made them bread. We even had some vegetables to eat. My health and spirits were slowly restored. I took care of the beans and turnips and other vegetables planted in our garden, and the children began to eat better.

Unfortunately, the Nationalists left after only a month and Communist troops came back again. They too stayed in part of our house. Repeatedly they asked me about my husband, what he did, where he was, and why he did not return. I told them that he studied theology in Mukden. One of them acted just like a thief, searching here and there. Although I tried to conceal some English books which were still on the bookshelves, he saw them.

'Your husband is pro-American,' he said. 'Where did he get so many English books?'

'Anybody can learn,' I replied. 'You also know English and are not pro-American.'

Obviously he did not believe me, so I had to fool him again, saying that we had received those English books and dictionaries from some rich people who had fled. Still he did not believe me. He continued to search our home and to inquire of the neighbours about us, but he got no information from them.

\* \* \* \* \* \*

All this time there were no letters from Charles. Then, during the New Year period of 1948, the Nationalist forces suddenly came back, and Charles came with them. But it was only a fleeting visit. A few days later they moved out and he left with them. He saw that the family was safe and well, and this gave him heart-peace, but when he set off for Mukden, we did not know when we would see each other again.

As soon as the Nationalists left, the Communists returned. This time they lit fires everywhere they went, tearing up railway tracks and pulling up wooden electricity poles. The railway sleepers which they tore up were useful as firewood; there was tar on the wood and it burned easily.

Ted and Jonathan went with others to pick up these sleepers for fuel. One day they told me they were going to carry home an electric pole. I was sure that such a long pole would be too heavy for them, but they went anyway, after striking a bargain with the two sons of Mr. Lee, the tanner, that the four of them would carry this pole home together and divide it equally among them.

The Lee boys were bigger and taller than Ted and Jonathan, but they wanted our boys to carry the thicker end of the pole. Since they had carried the heavy end home, Ted and Jonathan claimed that that end belonged to them. The Lee boys disagreed and there was a fight.

I came out and saw that my sons were very tired. 'Don't fight,' I said. 'Take whatever they give you.'

But Ted refused to give up. He sawed the pole in half and took the thicker half!

It was when Ted was walking around the sawn-off electric pole that he stumbled and fell over a half-frozen corpse, a victim of recent fighting. When he realised it was a dead body, he was terrified and what with fright and over-tiredness, he could not sleep at all that night. He told me that as soon as he closed his eyes he would see the pale face and the big foot of the dead man. He begged me not to blow out the lamp. But the next day both boys were back in the fields again picking soy beans!

\* \* \* \* \* \*

About this time an old fellow named Chi came from Tsitsihar. Originally from Chungku, he had become rich in Tsitsihar where he was the owner of a big oil press. But because of the Communist revolution he fled with all his wealth and came to our town. In his search for a place to stay, he stopped at our house.

'Since your husband is not at home,' he said, 'why don't you get a tenant?'

'Oh, that would be wonderful! If you don't think that our home is too shabby, you are welcome to use our north room.'

'How much should I pay?'

'Oh, nothing. Indeed, I would give you money to stay here if I had it! I live alone here with my seven children and am always in a state of fear. If you stay, the soldiers won't come. They might only ask me to cook for them, or things like that.'

So he agreed to move in - not just himself, but his wife, his son, his daughter-in-law, and his grand-daughter! I was delighted! It was a great boost to my flagging spirits.

Although the Communists now no longer stayed in our home, they did cook their meals there. Their cook was a captured Nationalist soldier, an educated man and a good man whose only duty was to cook three meals a day for this group of soldiers. During his leisure time, he often told us stories about the war and about the way the Communist troops had treated him. Each time he finished cooking a meal he would invite our two families to eat with him, so that we did not need to cook for ourselves. Even though the Communists stayed for more than two months on this occasion, we ate well and were not as afraid as we had been.

One day they came to look for stretcher-bearers. Old Mr. Chi's son was just over thirty years of age, an ideal candidate for such forced labour. We told him to lie down under the bedding below the feet of the women and children lying there so that he would not be discovered. The Communists arrived, poking their guns against the bed covers.

'Ouch!' I cried. 'Why are you poking that gun at us?'

'Just to find out if your are hiding a man there.'

'There is no man here. We are all women. The only man here is a ten-year-old boy. What can *he* do for you?'

They said nothing and left. But they were very sneaky. They hid at the back of the house to listen to what we might say. Then they came back. We were scared stiff.

'Look,' I said, 'we don't have any men here. We are all women and children. My husband is studying at Mukden and he will not be coming back. Please don't bother us any more.' This time they did go away.

After this search, Mr. Chi was frightened for his only son. Early the next morning, he and the son, also disguised as an old man, took a basket and went out ostensibly to pick up manure in the fields. The grandson carried a little bag and followed the men. Thus they escaped to Mukden.

The Communists stayed on with us in the day-time, and the Nationalists attacked at night. Now we women and children had to survive alone.

A month later Old Chi came back by himself. He said that he had come to take his wife, daughter-in-law and his grand-daughter back to Mukden.

What would I do now, I asked myself, with seven children in this house all by myself?

Just before they left, Old Chi said to me: 'I can see that all the decent people and the well-to-do have left this town. The rest who have stayed are not the good kind. Your husband is pro-American and he knows English. After we leave, your danger will surely increase. Those around you are watching you every day, and they'll rob you if they have an opportunity. Take my advice, my child, and leave this place. I know that your parents' place is only eight miles away, but for the safety of your seven children I think that you should leave as soon as possible. Don't worry about your house and your belongings. Don't try to take a lot of things with you. Just leave!'

* * * * * *

Although I did appreciate old Mr. Chi's advice and his good will, his words did nothing to relieve me of fear. I had no idea what I should do. My father was informed that we would be moving to his home, and one of my sisters and her husband helped us pack.

Long before the Communists came to our area I had started, as I have said, to store up food for an emergency. We had ten big sacks of grain, never discovered by searching soldiers and I really thanked God for hearing my prayer concerning this. After I gave birth to Bill, I always asked God to supply according to our needs. Communists came persistently asking for grain. Now that we were moving we had to get those ten sacks of grain out and away. God performed a miracle for us, for not one single Communist showed up that day!

At dusk my father arrived with a horse cart. We had a fairly large house with many poor people living in our downstairs and front rooms. But nobody heard the cart come and at midnight we loaded the grain and other things, expecting to come back the next day to pick up the rest. Just as we started out on the road a storm burst. I have never seen such large hail stones. However, by dawn, we had safely transported the ten sacks of grain.

The next day neighbours came in full of questions. Some mentioned the terrible mess our house was in; others guessed that we were moving grain; some said they had heard a cart in the night. I gave nothing away. All I wanted to do was to move to my father's home.

It was dark when my sister and I took the children and started walking down the road. Communist soldiers were stationed all along the way, but they did not bother us since we were only women and children. Jonathan carried Harry on his back; I held Bill in my arms, and the girls followed their aunt. We had to cross a small stream and a big river. The stream did not present too much of a problem: we just held the smaller children in our arms and walked across it hand-in-hand. But the big river was not so easy.

Originally the Japanese had built a bridge across it, but it had been bombed during the war and we could only walk in the water along the remaining wreckage. We were thoroughly soaked. My father was already waiting for us with his cart and took us to his home. It was located in an area of 'no man's land' - the Nationalists were there one day and the Communists another. I felt much more secure here with my grandmother, my father, my younger brother, three of my younger sisters and my own family around me.

* * * * * *

Now I had to find out where Charles was. Ten days after our drenched arrival, my youngest sister and I resolved to go to Rev. Feng at Tiehling who had been Charles' room-mate at the seminary. Rev. and Mrs. Feng were most compassionate and eager to help, and as I recounted our experiences, Mrs. Feng wept with me.

'Charles was wrong to do this,' said Mr. Feng. 'Of course, he was fleeing for his life, but it wasn't right to leave his wife and children behind.' He would write him immediately, he said.

I too wrote a letter telling Charles about our situation. I went back home after a couple of weeks while my sister stayed on, undertaking to pick up any mail from Charles which might arrive at Mr. Feng's home.

When my sister did come home, she was carrying a letter mailed in Shanghai. I was overjoyed when I saw its contents. Charles had not left us behind and gone to the United States by himself - on the contrary, he wanted us to come and be with him in Shanghai!

But doubt arose and discouragement set in. How could I get to Shanghai with seven children and no man to help me? The route to Shanghai was very dangerous. What if something should happen to the children on the way? But it was eldest son, Ted, who said, 'If you don't go, I'll go by myself.'

Again I wrote to Charles. A week went by and still we heard nothing. I became worried. At the end of the second week, I went to Tiehling and called on Rev. Feng to learn that a letter from Charles had just arrived at his home! It said, 'If you can get to Mukden, there is a plane there to bring you to Shanghai.'

Because of the war conditions, I had no idea

about how to get to Mukden nor did I know how to prepare for the trip. Instead of bringing hope, the letter brought us nothing but despair even if it did say: 'If God so wills, he will have a way to lead you out. There is nothing impossible with him.' Rev. Feng led us in prayer and tried to cheer me up. He said, 'We depend on God for everything. He will open the way for you.'

'Yes,' I thought, 'we ought to look to our God and keep silent. God leads us; we must be happy to follow.'

* * * * * *

Back at my father's house in Shantoupao a month went by. Early one morning my brother-in-law brought a telegram. It was from Charles and it simply said: GET TO MUKDEN ON THURSDAY. I couldn't tell which Thursday he was referring to. That very day was a Thursday, so I imagined this was probably the day. From Rev. Feng came another letter which he had received from Charles. It said, 'You must get to Mukden by Thursday afternoon. A plane will take off at six o'clock Friday morning. If you miss this, there will be no second chance. I trust God to open the way for you.'

My heart almost failed me. We were nervous, excited and elated, all at the same time. I hurriedly began packing. My father ran to tell my sister and her husband that we were leaving, and he borrowed their small cart. Pastor Liu said, 'Since we have committed all this to God, you need not worry any more. It is already dark. The Tiehling gate must be closed by now, so you cannot get in the city anyway. It will be dangerous for you to roam around with seven children. Wait till morning.'

Nobody could sleep well that night. My uncle was out spying on the Communists for me, and just before dawn he came in. 'You can go now,' he said. 'The Communists have left.' My father was urging me on. We put sacks of grain on the cart hoping to sell it for cash in Tiehling. My sister and brother-in-law drove the horse cart for us.

My father especially loved my husband. Before we left he said to me, 'My daughter, do not try to hinder your husband from going to America to study. If you find a peaceful place to live and the children have enough to eat, that will be good enough.'

My father and uncle followed us, running alongside the cart. 'Please go back now,' I said, as I waved goodbye. My father and my sister were crying, but - I don't know why - my eyes had no tears. There were two carts, one carrying the sacks of grain, the other carrying the people. The carts rolled along faster and faster, and fifteen miles on we reached

Nationalist-controlled territory. All along the way the Nationalist soldiers insisted on inspecting us and our carts of grain.

'Would you please hurry?' I pleaded. 'We have to catch a train. My husband is waiting for us in Shanghai.' One soldier believed me and let us pass.

I have no idea how many inspection points we went through, and when we entered the city of Tiehling, the inspections became even more thorough. They told us that once we brought grain into the city we could not bring it back out, so I asked my sister and brother-in-law to take the grain out and sell it for us.

With the children, I went to visit Rev. Feng, who was delighted to see us. At noon, we were still counting the money from the sale of the grain; at noon also the only train that day to Mukden was due to leave. A cousin of Charles by marriage had been looking after the exchange of our money. 'Don't worry,' he said. 'My son is a doctor and the station-master is one of his patients. I told him to go and buy your tickets, and he will see that your train does not leave before you get there.'

At one o'clock in the afternoon we were still counting. I was becoming desperate. 'Don't count any more money! I'll take whatever is there!' Picking up the bags of money, we ran to the station.

There Charles' cousin urged us to board the train quickly.

As we climbed up the steps the train began to move. He thrust the tickets into my hand through the window and we were off. I shall never be able to thank that man enough! Is not the grace of God truly wonderful? How we ought always to rely on God for everything! That way he will make us prosper.

* * * * * *

The train took four hours to reach Mukden. Rev. Feng found a carriage and we drove immediately to the Manchuria Council Hall, local office of the Lutheran Conference. There we were met by Mr. Chang, the clerk. 'Are you Mrs. Charles Chao?'

'Yes, I am.'

'Have you brought all your seven children?'

'Yes, I have. How do you know so much about us?' Apparently he already had all our names on a list prepared by Charles in Shanghai.

'I am in charge of the plane and all the departures from the airport. You should really thank God. This plane was to have taken off this morning, but mechanical problems developed to delay the flight. It will not leave for about four more days. We have to wait for some parts to be shipped in from Shanghai.'

My heart overflowed with gratitude and praise! This had been God's plan for opening up a way for us. Surely we can never fully comprehend the mercy of our heavenly Father. Suddenly I saw light streaming into the darkness, and this experience of God's miraculous ways was instrumental in wonderfully strengthening my personal faith.

Mr. Chang invited us to stay at the mission headquarters. I was afraid that I had too many children and that they would create problems for the employees, so I offered to go and stay with a cousin I knew locally. This cousin seemed to welcome us, but his wife was a bit reluctant. To be honest, I did not blame her; it is not easy to entertain a mother and seven children in time of war. But we had no choice, we stayed, and his wife turned out to be very kind to us.

Next day, as the children were playing outside, I overheard from next door a conversation between a Chinese doctor and his wife: 'Old Juo next door is really unlucky,' he was saying. 'The Chao family are staying with him - seven children and one adult. You can guess the amount of food they'll eat every day!'

'They're waiting for a plane, and they'll be here only four days.'

'You women are too ready to believe what people say. I doubt whether they'll ever leave.

There's no food at Chungku where they come from, so they've come here to get some. I don't think they will ever leave, even if he tries to push them out.'

The man's words saddened my heart. 'Lord,' I prayed, 'may you be glorified. Do not let your handmaid be ashamed. I do not blame the man for talking this way, but I trust in you completely, for you are an Almighty God. Nothing is impossible for you.' Thereupon I dismissed his words from my mind.

Next day, at three o'clock in the afternoon, Mr. Chang from the Lutheran Mission arrived. I was to report to the mission headquarters before six o'clock where all passengers had to gather for their luggage to be weighed. Our plane would take off for Shanghai at dawn the next day.

'I've managed to exchange your bag of money for $105 in American money.'

I thanked him. 'Except for your help, I would never have known how to hide that bag.'

'It was all done by the grace of God,' he said.

We took off at five o'clock the next morning and flew directly to Shanghai. I felt a deep sense of gratitude to God for his grace and his providence. My faith was like a fool's faith, who believes without too much thought or rationalisation. I boarded this plane with my seven children without even knowing an address or telephone number to reach my husband in Shanghai. When Charles wrote and told me to come to Mukden, I went immediately by faith and never stopped to think, 'What if there is no place for us there?' After we left my father's place, I had sold all our precious grain and beans for cash, never thinking whether or not we would need those stores in the future. Yet it so turned out that we could now see how, without our knowledge, God had planned the whole escape.

As the plane taxied along the runway at Shanghai airport, Sam spotted his father through the little window. 'Look, Mum, Daddy is out there waiting for us!'

It was an emotional reunion. We were together at last!

## 12

*That he may do his work, his strange work*
*(Isaiah 28:21)*

Before my family reached Shanghai in May 1948,
all the preparations for my own trip to the United
States to study at Faith University had been completed.

But because of the weeks of uncertainty over my
family's escape from Communist Manchuria, I realised that alternative arrangements would have to
be ready in the event that God did bring them out.
So it was that I sought the Lord's will regarding an
opportunity to serve him somewhere in China.

My friend, Rev. Egbert Andrews, of the Orthodox Presbyterian Church introduced me to Rev.
Albert Smit of the Christian Reformed Church
Mission in the district of Rukao, north of Shanghai. We found that we got on well together. Most
of Mr. Smit's workers were over fifty years of age.

'You are young, and your English is quite good,'
he said. 'You are welcome to join us and to work
in the field of Christian literature.'

I explained that I was still waiting to see whether my family would get out of Manchuria, and told him quite frankly that my working with his Mission depended on that; if there was no way for them to leave, then I would go on as planned to study in America.

Mr. Smit saw no problem. He was willing to wait. So when my family, by the Lord's hand, managed to catch that Lutheran mercy plane at Mukden, my plan to go abroad was automatically cancelled. I took this as the Lord's leading and set my mind to working in the Christian Reformed Mission at Rukao.

On the very day that my family and I were reunited at Shanghai airport, Mr. Smit had already made plans for me to meet the people at Rukao where I would preach to see if they considered me suitable. I saw the family comfortably settled in the Mindefang Christian refugee hostel for wives and children of Chinese preachers who had had to flee from Communist areas. Then Mr. Smit and I travelled to Rukao by river steamboat and taxi. I preached my trial sermon and the people seemed satisfied with me. But soon I found myself re-entering 'The Tiger's Mouth'.

I hurried back to Shanghai for the family and on the way back had to rent a car for the last lap to Rukao. We stopped for petrol at one point and the proprietor of the filling station noted that my accent was not local. I explained, and said that I was on my way to Rukao. 'What?' he said. 'That's a Communist area!'

His comment immediately troubled my wife.

'We have just fled from one Communist zone and now we enter another! We'd better get back to Shanghai right away.'

'I have promised the Rukao church that I will work there; we can't go back; we'll have to try it out, anyway.'

Back at Rukao we were put in a rented hotel room until the preacher's house could be cleared of other refugees and made ready for us. Mr. Smit had it freshly whitewashed and a new kitchen was built on. But there was murmuring within the congregation: former preachers had never been treated so generously. Although Mr. Smit was doing all he could to make my family comfortable, there was extreme jealously among the other preachers and their wives. And it showed. When Mr. Smit left for his summer break, another preacher, Mr. Wang, didn't bother to introduce us to the congregation: he took it upon himself to lead all the worship services and prayer meetings. We were left completely out of the picture.

The background to all this was explained to us by another member of the flock. The Wangs, he said, were desperate to remain at Rukao instead of being moved by the Mission Board to other work. That the newly-repaired house had been given to me did not help matters.

So what with the trouble which the Wangs created for us in the church and the difficulty that the family had in adjusting to a very hot summer in a lowland basin, we felt that this was not after all the place for us. I wrote to Mr. Smit to this effect and he broke his vacation to deal with the problem. It was agreed that I should change places with Mr. Hsia at Paipu in the same district; there, at a higher altitude, the summer was pleasantly cool.

The Paipu church had started life as a large temple. In the course of a government campaign to break up 'superstition', it had been converted to a district administrative office. With the arrival of foreigners - all of whom were assumed to be wealthy - it was put up for sale. American missionaries saw it, liked it, and bought it. It had been well adapted to provide plenty of space for worship and accommodation.

To begin with I inherited the difficulties faced by earlier foreign missionaries - few believers, and not an educated person among them. However, I pressed on with visitation. Then some doctors came to the church. One of them was Dr. Tsao: his father had been a preacher, although the doctor himself had not attended church since beginning his medical practice. After I had visited him, not only he but his whole family returned to the house of God. And so life in the church gradually revived and we started evangelistic work in the country-side.

One day, after dinner, Miss Goutes, the American missionary, her assistant Miss Liu, and I were chatting about the general situation. Miss Liu described how local Communist guerillas often came to make trouble: a district official had been beheaded by them, and the town talked for long about it.

'If you hear a knock at your door at night,' she said, 'don't open it.'

At midnight that very night, we were all aroused by hammering on the door. As we held back from opening it, the knocking stopped and a voice yelled, 'Open up! We're police and National Army. We're from District Headquarters. We want to check who lives here!'

With some relief I opened the door. The first man in was indeed in Nationalist uniform.

'Why did you take so long to open the door!'

'Why do you knock in such a manner?'

He didn't answer. They did a routine check of the registration book and didn't bother with a house search.

But suddenly it dawned on me that they had merely come to make trouble. I recognised the one in uniform: he had come into the church that day and had sat down at the piano to play hit tunes. I had challenged him. 'The church piano is used only for the church services - not for playing popular music.' This night visit was by way of being his revenge. He had to go to all this trouble to demonstrate his 'power' and to recover 'face'. How treacherous the human heart!

While still at Rukao, I had received a letter from Rev. Samuel E. Boyle in Canton. He had learned from Dr. Vos and Dr. Boettner that I had mean-time given up the idea of studying in America. Would I come to the south to assist him in begin-ning to translate Reformed theological works into Chinese?

'This plan was conceived by me alone,' he wrote. 'I do not have any mission board to back me financially. We must do it entirely by faith.'

I had replied immediately after conferring with Mr. Smit, who had pressed me to stay.

'We have translation work to do in our denomi-nation too,' he said. 'The situation here isn't too bad. The big cities are still in the hands of the Nationalists.'

I found it hard to forget his previous kindness to me and felt I had no option but to stay. I was soon to be moved to Paipu where I settled down for a while at least.

But the Civil War escalated. The Nationalist forces were in a perilous position. There came the day that I took a bus to Rukao to see Mr. Smit to tell him of our intention to leave. But he had gone to Shanghai, intending to call on me at Paipu on the way. I had missed him. There was general confusion on the outskirts of Rukao, with every sign of retreat: crowds of military dependants loaded with parcels and baggage of all kinds were waiting to board military vehicles. I merged with them and boarded a truck. At Paipu I jumped off and went home.

Mr. Smit had in fact called, and had left a sum of money, indicating that if we wanted to go to Shanghai, this was a good time to go; but if we wanted to stay, we could stay.

I told my wife to get ready to leave immediately. She even packed clothes which were still wet from the wash. I ordered a rented car for the next morning and in spite of a last-minute effort by Miss Liu to persuade us to stay, we left the Paipu church where we had started work barely four months before.

## 13

*My unfailing love for you will not be shaken
(Isaiah 54:10)*

Samuel E. Boyle was a missionary of the Reformed Presbyterian Church of North America who had served in Kuangtung Province since 1934. During his missionary work he was aware of the world wide crisis concerning liberal theology in the Christian Church. He was distressed by the growing number of Chinese translations of the 'New Theology' as Modernism was called in China, and the lack of authoritative Chinese books to defend the true faith. Driven by a sense of urgency, Rev. Boyle determined to start some kind of Christian translation work producing sound Reformed theological books for China.

In China during the Sino-Japanese War he had met a Christian university teacher, Mr. Hon Ka Lai, who had translated into Chinese J. Gresham Machen's book, *Christianity and Liberalism.* When Rev. Boyle returned to America in 1941, he carried this Chinese translation manuscript home with him as a great treasure, and although the Pacific War delayed his return to South China until 1947, he brought the Machen manuscript back to China with him then.

As soon as we reached Shanghai, I again wrote to Mr. Boyle, enclosing with the letter a group picture of my family. He later told me that when he saw that picture he was startled, for the living expenses of a family of nine people posed a big problem in Canton at the time.

Before Christmas 1948, Mr. Boyle's wife received a gift of $60 in US money from her brother; this the Boyles put at our disposal to help pay our passage to Canton. In late December, we sailed from Shanghai for South China and Canton.

Our family travelled in the cargo-hold of the SS *Chingkang*. It carried many refugees, all having to sleep shoulder-to-shoulder on their straw mats. Luggage was heaped at one side. The food was barely edible. My wife suffered from seasickness.

The ship's captain, on his first voyage to Canton, was not familiar with the harbour. Young and stubborn, he refused to pay $60 for a pilot. As we groped our way in, the vessel ran aground.

The passengers yelled their complaints at the captain for his tight-fisted attitude. All this noise and strife I stood back from, knowing that all the shouting would get us nowhere. I knelt there and prayed for God's deliverance.

We spent Christmas Day on the ship, then it was announced that the tide was flooding back. We thanked God for safe arrival at Whangpo harbour.

It was the first time we had set foot in South China and we were thrilled. There was a fresh novelty in all that we saw and heard. All around were trees, flowers, grass lawns, fields - so seldom seen in the north at this season and all a delight to our eyes. Instead of the tense anxiety on the faces of people in the north, we experienced here serenity and confidence. It was indeed a free and pleasant land. Surely no Communists could ever come here.

We headed for the residence of Rev. Peter Soong, pastor of a Covenanter Church. After a brief wait, I at last found myself talking face-to-face with the man with whom for months I had been having spiritual fellowship - the Rev. Samuel E. Boyle.

The American Reformed Presbyterian Mission had bought a business property in Canton and converted it into a place of worship with accommodation attached. Here, on the second floor and upstairs from the chapel, was our home.

Everything in the city was new to us. We could neither speak nor understand the Cantonese dialect and had all kinds of problems - especially when trying to shop in the market. At this time, Dr. Boyle introduced us to Mrs. Jeanette Li, well known for her book, *The Lord's Grace is Sufficient*. She had learned our family's Manchurian dialect when she worked in the north with Dr. Vos. We became friends, and she was a great help to us in Canton when we went to buy food, kitchen utensils and other commodities.

This ignorance of Cantonese caused other problems, too. At a church service we could understand only a few words, such as 'Jesus Christ'. Everything else was 'Greek' to us! But I did try to learn the dialect. I went to classes at the local YMCA and began to come to terms with the nine basic tones of Cantonese - so difficult for us who knew only the four tones of Mandarin. These nine tones have to be pitched accurately, otherwise the whole meaning of a word or phrase can be changed. One day, talking to a young man in the church, I decided to try out my Cantonese. I wanted to express the idea of applying or putting into practice - 'shat hang' - but my pronunciation was off the mark: when I used the term 'shih hang' the young fellow exploded with laughter. I had actually used the word for 'dung-hill' - a coarse expression in Cantonese!

But with study, my understanding increased. Soon I could follow the preacher with my Chinese Bible open, and could understand most of the sermon; I could even converse a little. So far, however, I was not able to preach in the dialect. One day I did preach, but in Mandarin, while Pastor Soong interpreted in Cantonese. After the service, Mr. Boyle came forward. He shook my hand. 'I have often listened recently to Chinese co-workers preach, but I have never been so moved as I was today. Your preaching of the Reformed Faith shows how you have been influenced by J.G. Vos.' That compliment did much to encourage me at the time.

There was a printing office next door to our church. I had a chat one day with the owner. 'Can you print magazines and periodicals?' He assured me that he could, and with an idea already in my mind I asked for prices. I wanted to publish a magazine. Printing costs should not be excessive and Dr. Boyle was in full agreement with the idea. And so, in 1949, *Reformation Faith* was launched as a bi-monthly enterprise. Later it would be called *The Reformed Faith* and was the forerunner of our present Reformation Translation Fellowship magazine, *Reformed Faith and Life*.

We mailed copies of the first edition as far away as Mukden and Yingtou. Many letters came back expressing appreciation of the contents and of how people had been helped by reading them.

They found their way into the hands of the

students at the China Theological Seminary in Shanghai, and it was at their suggestion that in 1950 the name was changed to *Faith and Life*; the Chinese characters for 'reform', they said, had a bad connotation in the church then - a socialistic flavour. At first, *Reformation Faith* was sent out free of charge. But clearly money would be needed for this and for the other areas of translation and publishing. Dr. Boyle, therefore, sent a prayer letter to friends in the US appealing for support in prayer and gifts. God did not let us down. We have never wanted for money since that first letter.

Meanwhile I continued my translation work. I worked on the Chinese translation of J. Gresham Machen's *Christianity and Liberalism*, correcting the manuscript and preparing it for publication. I continued work begun when I was with UNRRA at Mukden on my translation of Boettner's *The Reformed Doctrine of Predestination*. So my ministry in literature work continued in Canton, combined with some preaching at the church there.

But in the spring of 1949, the war news from the north was ominous. Evacuation of all foreign workers in the Reformed Presbyterian Mission was decided upon. Off went the Boyles to Hong Kong on August 8th, with Mrs. Boyle expecting her third child which was born on August 9th, the day after they arrived.

By September most of the foreign missionaries were gone. Our family remained in our second floor apartment above the chapel. Letters came from Mr. Boyle: one contained Hong Kong money and in it he urged me to move as soon as possible. The Liberation Army of the Communists was driving steadily southwards with little effective Nationalist resistance. Still I took all this to be merely rumour: surely South China would not fall so easily.

But Mr. Boyle's political vision was clearer than mine. When I realised that Rev. Peter Soong himself was planning to move to Hong Kong, I acted on the plea in Mr. Boyle's letter and Mr. Soong and I left together - Mr. Soong with his family and I by myself.

'Why did you come alone?' Mr. Boyle was clearly upset.

I explained that I knew nothing about Hong Kong and had assumed that arriving with my whole family - nine people - would have caused problems. Mr. Boyle had indeed intended us all to come together: that was what he had sent the money for. But next morning he showed true understanding and friendship.

Yes, he agreed, there might have been housing problems; but he was still anxious for the whole family to come to Hong Kong.

Back I went to Canton. We pondered on the proposed move. The cost of living was high in the Colony; how could we afford to live in such a place? We couldn't afford to entertain such fancy notions. We had always seen Canton as the last stop in our flight from Communism; anything after that would have to be committed into God's hands.

But the old Chinese saying had become a reality to us: 'When one comes to the edge of the mountain or the end of a stream, one wonders where he can go after that. But then a new village is revealed through the shadowy willow path and the bright flowery trail.'

We started preparations to leave. Our two eldest sons would join us at the end of the term from their Christian primary school.

Then one day Dr. Boyle arrived. The good man pretended that he had come on Mission business but I learned later that he had come specifically to help us move. 'I've found you a place to stay in Hong Kong. I had to come to Canton on business, so I might as well help you.'

We were on the boat for Hong Kong the next day. Our belongings were few, and Mr. Boyle was not slow to take off his jacket and roll up his sleeves as we moved the baggage. He treated us like his own brothers. Our ignorance of Cantonese could again have been a problem at the Hong Kong docks: we were open to abuse and dishonesty at the hands of the coolies who worked there. Another Chinese proverb runs: 'There are five classes of people who need to be killed, even if they are innocent: the people who rent carts, the boat people, the inn-keepers, the coolies and the clerks in a court of law.' Things have not changed much since then!

But it was Mr. Boyle who met the coolies with his fluent Cantonese: they dared not pull any tricks, but carried our entire baggage from the boat to the ferry-pier where we would leave for Cheung Chau Island.

I thanked God for his wonderful grace. And surely I will never forget the brotherly love of Samuel E. Boyle and all that he did for our family!

As well as Hong Kong's main island, there are many smaller islands off the 'New Territories' of the mainland. Among these is Cheung Chau - Long Island - about an hour by ferry from Hong Kong. Over the years, the hilly part of it had been developed as a summer resort by missionaries; down at sea-level, it was a crowded Chinese city clustered along the harbour.

Number 1, East Bay was our rented accommodation down by the beach. There we were, eight people packed into the little back room of a small house - the two of us, five children, and Ah Kwan, the Cantonese maid we had brought from Canton to help my wife with the children. At night we slept on wooden bed-boards with a partition hung across the room to make two sleeping areas.

The day we arrived, it was raining. Mr. Boyle had helped us to get settled in while his wife, up the hill in their rented house, prepared a big pot of rice and a large dish of meat to go with it. These Mr. Boyle carried down in the rain - with no spare hand for an umbrella! He had also taken a hammer to help us hang up the mosquito nets over our 'beds'.

'Who was he?' asked Mr. Tang, the owner of the house.

'That,' I said, 'was Mr. Boyle, our American co-worker.'

'I've never seen a foreigner treat his Chinese co-workers like that,' replied Mr. Tang. 'He is truly a man full of love.'

Every morning at nine o'clock, I used to walk up the hill to Mr. Boyle's cottage, and there we began work on the revision of Machen's *Christianity and Liberalism*. It was, we knew, an important book and we truly felt the presence of God as we worked together on it.

All this time, the newspapers reported the steady advance of the Communists and the imminent danger to Canton. Mr. Boyle was sure that I should return to Canton for my two sons at the Christian primary school.

Once again I relied on Mr. Boyle to help me with my travel. He was accustomed to elbowing his way through a seething crowd like the one at Kowloon station, and soon had my ticket for Canton. I fetched the boys from the school and we managed to book a passage on the very last river boat to leave before the city was lost to the Communists. It was a narrow escape!

Ever since we had reached Hong Kong with our large family, the burden of the cost to Mr. Boyle had been great. We had no financial backing and the Reformed Presbyterian Mission had no provision in its budget for our expenses. So far, four issues of the *Reformation Faith* had gone out, so Mr. Boyle wrote to Dr. J.G. Vos in the United States asking him to form a non-profit-making voluntary association. It would be called 'The Reformation Translation Fellowship Incorporated'.

*Christianity and Liberalism* was finally published in 1951. The first edition of 5000 copies soon disappeared, largely as a result of great demand from readers in Communist China who took advantage of our offer of free copies.

As well as the publication of Chinese books and pamphlets, other work that year included gathering information from the Chinese press and other sources so that Mr. Boyle could write an English book on the changing situation of the Christian Church in Communist China. The book, *The Church in Red China Leans to One Side,* received favourable reviews in America and even Holland. This was yet another by-product of our main ministry - the preparation of Reformed theological works in Chinese. Through it, the West was informed of persecution under Communism.

## 14

*Direct me in the path of your commands
(Psalm 119:35)*

By 1950, the American Reformed Presbyterian Church was moving with the tide of evangelical interest in post-war Japan. Under General Mac-Arthur's liberal military occupation, Christian missions were openly welcomed to minister to the defeated nation.

But for the South China Mission in Hong Kong the decision to move into Japan was not easy. In February 1950 Mr. Boyle was officially sent to Japan on a fact-finding trip: he would talk with other denominations and with Japanese Christians about the possibility of opening a Reformed Presbyterian Mission there. As far as the Reformed Presbyterian Church in America was concerned, this was not to be seen as the desertion of China, but as a step further forward. The Reformed Presbyterian Synod had always fully endorsed our work - the literary evangelism, the magazine and the translation work.

Mr. Boyle was in Japan for two weeks. The needs and opportunities, he decided, were clear. He recommended to the American Synod that the South China Mission be temporarily closed and that a new mission be opened in Kobe, Japan. Here and in Osaka lived many Chinese who spoke Cantonese.

In March, the Board of Foreign Missions in America, formally decided to agree to his recommendation. The Boyles and some others would 'open at some appropriate centre' while the South China headquarters would remain as long as possible 'to keep in touch with the Chinese Church on the mainland'.

Mr. Boyle and family and two co-workers arrived at Nagoya on July 17th. He had already seen the possibility of this new ministry involving me and my family: I could speak Japanese and some Cantonese; the R.T.F. might operate from Kobe, maintaining the Chinese work through literature. And so it was that he urged me to go to Japan.

At the time I felt no zest for moving: my family was large, our eighth child, Grace, was born in September; it seemed best to stay in Hong Kong. But still Mr. Boyle's persistent letters kept arriving: there was accommodation; the Mission had rented a foreign-style hillside house west of Kobe.

Yet, this kind man with loving heart did not conceal the difficulties, much as he wanted us to join him. How well I knew him as a result of our close fellowship! He once described himself to me by a Chinese idiom - 'the head of a tiger but the tail of a snake' (great ambitions but small achievements!)

At the time, too, I was in touch with Rev. Egbert Andrews, our friend from Shanghai, who was now in Taiwan, as was another friend, Rev. James Montgomery, working with the China Sunday School Association. I went so far as to buy some 'patriotic Bonds' from the Taiwan Government; without these, I had heard, nobody could enter Taiwan.

But in December we received news that my entry to Japan had been approved by the Republic of China delegation in Tokyo. My mind had been made up for me. Three days before Christmas, we set sail on a Swedish freighter which had a few passenger cabins - quite a difference from our Shanghai to Canton voyage in 1948: good food, a dining hall - and beds! We called at Taiwan, Yokohama, Osaka and finally, Kobe, where there awaited us a telegram of welcome from Samuel Boyle!

\* \* \* \* \* \*

Our first sight of post-war Japan was frightening and depressing: wrecked buildings reminded us of the tragedy of war.

We had brought with us some commodities that Mr. Boyle had suggested in his letters, things like powdered milk and coffee. The customs inspector said, 'You certainly have a lot of coffee here! Could I have some?' No such foreign luxuries could be brought into Japan at the time. But he was quite understanding when I said I was sorry but I was bringing the coffee at the request of a friend.

Mr. Boyle and his family lived in the Kobe suburb of Suma, and we were to stay next door to him. From the house half-way up a hill, we looked down on the main line of the National Railway and beyond that there was a magnificent view of the ocean shore and the waters of Osaka Bay. Suma itself was at sea level. Our new home was spacious with several rooms and a kitchen; there was a sizeable garden and even a tennis court! But it was an old house: when it rained the roof leaked. Nevertheless, it was an idyllic setting: being neither poet nor artist, I cannot do justice to it!

The wonderful roominess enabled us to have an office for me, a meeting place for worship, and a dining-room. In these favourable circumstances, I resumed work on my translation of Boettner's volume on *Predestination,* while at the same time helping Mr. Boyle get under way with some neighbourhood evangelism among the Japanese.

The original plan - to concentrate on Cantonese and other Chinese in Kobe - had, however, to be dropped. This was out of consideration for the missionaries of the Southern Presbyterian Church of the United States: they had been first to come to Japan, and their Church had invested heavily in new work among the Chinese of Kobe. Our Reformed Presbyterian Mission therefore decided to change over to Japanese evangelism, and it was back to language school for our American missionaries. Mr. Boyle and I, although able to speak Japanese, did not feel well enough equipped to preach in the language, so at the church meetings in Mr. Boyle's house we used an interpreter.

As had been the case in Hong Kong, school was a problem in Japan. Ted was fourteen and Jonathan was twelve: they could not speak Japanese and so were debarred from the Japanese schools. In the end, we had them enrolled in Tung Wen School - the only Chinese school we could find in Kobe. Here the Nationalist Chinese flag flew outside, but inside was a hive of Communist activity. Even the headmaster was rumoured to be a leading figure in Communist circles.

The school was strongly hostile to religion. Our children, brought up in a Christian environment and within a Christian home, became the target of a small group of mockers among the pupils. On the day that the teacher touched on religion and invited opinions from the class, our Jonathan told the history of Christianity and delivered quite a sermon on its main doctrines. The teacher was baffled and offered no response! But that was the end of 'religious discussions' as far as the school management were concerned. For his own effort, Jonathan was reprimanded!

These and other incidents made us decide to look for some other place for the children. Ted and Jonathan, and later Bill, joined St. Michael's, a private Christian school run by the Church of England. The experience was new. All classes were in English: although Ted coped, Jonathan had more difficulty; what with his lack of familiarity with English and the fact that he had to leave many friends from the previous school, he was often downcast. But gradually he adjusted.

Bill was seven when he joined St. Michael's. That God's hand was upon our family was illustrated when Bill had an accident. On the way to school with Jonathan one day, he was struck by a lorry when its driver had tried to beat the red light. However, the accident was witnessed by Rev. James Tan of the nearby Presbyterian Church who took charge of the situation. Bill had been struck on the head but there was no haemorrhage. We committed him to the Lord in prayer. Evening came and he was still unconscious. The concerned lorry driver had waited with us all the time but we let him go: as Christians we felt that we should not press charges. Next day Bill slowly opened his eyes. In five days we had him home. Had he taken one step more that day, his whole body would have been crushed. How we thanked God for his grace in the protection of our family!

Although getting to school involved much travel for the children each day, they were at least in a Christian atmosphere and we could rest assured that they would not be contaminated by Communist-style education. After all, had we not spent most of our lives trying to escape from Communism as we ran from Manchuria to Central China, from Central China to South China and from South China to Japan?

On the domestic scene, things were hard for us on US$100 a month. There were ten mouths to feed - our family increased by two while we were in Kobe. Lois was born on the 4th, March, 1952 and Rose on 13th, June 1953. In addition, the children's rail travel to school in Osaka cost a small fortune. My pockets were always empty well before the next pay-day came round.

Among our American colleagues in Kobe was

Miss Rose Huston who had served the Lord for years in South China and later with the Reformed Presbyterian Mission at Tsitsihar, North Manchuria. She had been number nine, she told us, in a family of fourteen! With her experience of economic struggle within a large family, she had determined that when she grew up she would help other such families where she could. Just as her family had received much help when the children were small, so she now turned her compassionate efforts to us, and her constant concern and help were just like those of a close relative. She had learned to like Manchurian food, so every Lord's Day she would come from the city and share our jiaotze and noodles.

It was Miss Huston's idea that my wife start raising chickens. She provided the money for us to buy the first ten hens and some poultry feed. Soon the hens began to lay, and what eggs we did not need ourselves we sold to other regular customers, including some of the missionaries. Profits boomed! We increased our poultry stock to fifty and collected an average of twenty-six eggs a day. Now my wife had to care for eight children, fifty hens, one dog and one cat!

\* \* \* \* \* \*

Eventually I completed my translation of *The*

*Reformed Doctrine of Predestination*; such was its length in Chinese that it appeared in two volumes. It was a task during which I was deeply conscious of the grace of God.

At the same time, I continued to receive invitations to preach in Mandarin and English. One who often gave me such invitations was Mr. McLauchlin, a former missionary in China, who worked among the Chinese in Kobe. I also helped him start an English class. Of the many Chinese who came to learn English, there were those who were drawn, too, to the church, and we made many friends among them.

For one year of my stay in Japan, I studied at the Kobe Reformed Theological Seminary. The founding of the Seminary was the outcome of co-operation between the Southern Presbyterian Church of the US and a post-war denomination called the Reformed Church of Japan started by graduates of Philadelphia's Westminster Seminary. Here I studied the Old Testament under the influential Dr. William McIlwaine, son of missionaries and himself a noted missionary.

My best friend among my Japanese fellow students was a Mr. Hashimoto. He had graduated in Economics, but later suffered from poor health which led to mental depression. After he came to trust in the Lord Jesus, however, he changed completely to a happy man full of hope. His English was better than my Japanese, and on Saturdays we would talk and talk for hours together and share a Chinese meal. Later he became President of the Kobe Seminary.

I had always felt uneasy about the way people called me 'Reverend' Chao. True, I had taught and preached in many Chinese churches in Japan but I had never been ordained.

It was in 1954 that the Far East Commission of the Reformed Presbyterian Church of North America decided that, in view of my busy ministry and my literature work for China, I should be ordained. By May of that year I had completed six months of preparation for a comprehensive examination and passed in theology, exegesis and homiletics. I preached my ordination trial sermon in Kobe Reformed Seminary chapel, choosing for my text Hebrews 6:1-8. I was approved by the Commission, formally ordained in the presence of many friends, and became a minister of the Reformed Presbyterian Church of North America.

While I was in China and Manchuria, I had had no opportunity to study with a view to gaining entrance to an American theological college. This I had often regretted. Study in the Kobe Seminary had been difficult because lectures and discussions were in Japanese; but more than that, a Kobe qualification was not equivalent to the college or university degree which I would need to get into an American graduate seminary.

It was with these thoughts that at the end of my year at Kobe I went to Kwansei Gakuin University. The manner in which it was made possible showed once again God's hand at work.

At the time, two obstacles appeared to block the way: how could I afford the tuition fees, and what would now happen about my R.T.F. literature work? Once again, it was Samuel Boyle who came to my aid. The Boyles had always been enthusiastic about me seeking a degree, and now Mr. Boyle wrote a letter of recommendation to the University. He put my mind at ease, too, concerning the R.T.F. 'We know that all you hope to do,' he said, 'is to increase your ability to serve the Lord.' He also wrote to friends in America about my desire to study there, and funds for the purpose began to arrive; with that, and some money that my wife had saved for an emergency, I registered as a student. God is almighty: he knows our every need.

At the age of thirty-nine I wondered if I was too old to find studying easy; but I could not give up the hope of going to America. It was a very happy period of my life. My children and I used to board the same train each morning, they on their way to *their* school and me on my way to *mine,* carrying my bag of books just as in schoolboy days!

At the end of it all, I received a BA degree in English and American literature. Mr. Boyle, my wife, and daughter Rose, watched me graduate in June 1956.

## 15

*A door was opened to me by the Lord
(2 Corinthians 2:12)*

In August the same year, I sailed out of Kobe bound for Seattle and set foot on American soil on September 12th. I had come to America for further study: first at the Reformed Presbyterian Seminary in Pittsburgh for one year, and then to proceed to Westminster Seminary, Philadelphia.

For sixteen years I had enjoyed fellowship 'by correspondence' with Dr. Loraine Boettner, the man who had so encouraged me and through whose generosity I was now in the USA. My train reached Omaha before dawn and I had time, as I thought, for some sleep in a waiting-room. A man entered: he was just what I had imagined Dr. Boettner would look like.

'Dr. Boettner?'

'Yes. Mr. Chao? Welcome!'

He had got up at four in the morning to drive the seventy miles to pick me up.

During my short stay, I was much impressed by

his personality and life-style. Here was a foremost figure in the field, yet his home was plainly furnished and I found him a humble and kind man. He had never been ordained, partly because he had never found public speaking easy, but mainly because he felt that God had called him to a literary ministry.

Two interesting points about his writing are worth recording. He himself financed, in part, the publication of some of his earlier books, making them available at less than list price to seminary and Bible School students. As well as that, Dr. Boettner's books bear the following inscription:

> Anyone is at liberty to use material from this book, with or without credit. He himself has received help from many sources, some acknowledged and many unacknowledged. He believes the material herein contained to be a true statement of Scriptural truth, and his desire is to further, not to restrict its use.

It was with reluctance that I left Dr. Boettner's company, but also with a feeling of real satisfaction.

\* \* \* \* \* \*

Pittsburgh is the home of the Reformed Presbyterian Seminary, formerly the mansion of a wealthy merchant. Here I found myself assigned to sleep in the second floor students' dormitory. But even Seminary students can be noisy, and later I was allowed to have a single room!

I was talking one day to the Seminary's President, Dr. S. Bruce Willson, and the conversation came round to my family. I told him about how the eldest, Ted, was to come to America in September to start at Geneva College and about how the education of the other nine was a great burden to me. It was wishful thinking, I said, that my family might all come to America one day. The cost would be enormous. Dr. Willson's response was simple. 'Let us commit this matter to the Lord,' he said.

It was the time of the Reformed Presbyterian Synod and Rev. Samuel Boyle had come from Japan to attend. I brought up with him the question of my family's future. But the Synod would not be able to help; after all, the Reformation Translation Fellowship was a para-church fellowship and outside the Synod's budget. Mr.. Boyle estimated that it would take $5000 to bring my family to the USA. 'This Synod,' said Dr. Willson, 'would be very glad to sponsor your family's immigration if somebody were to put up $5000.' The matter, however, was dropped and did not come before the Synod.

En route from Seattle to Omaha and my meeting Dr. Boettner, I had enjoyed a short visit with

Rev. Lester E. Kilpatrick who was the American representative of the Reformation Translation Fellowship. He it was who now arranged a summer tour for me in order to promote the work of the R.T.F. by speaking at churches spanning the country from Pittsburgh to California.

My first stop was Chicago where the pastor of the Reformed Presbyterian Church, Philip Coon, placed adverts in the local press, announcing that Mr. Chao, a Chinese pastor, would tell of his family's escape from Communism. The adverts brought a number of visitors from other churches. As I stood at the door with Mr. Coon shaking hands with the people as they left, a tall stranger stopped to talk.

'Where is your family now? In Pittsburgh?'

'No, I am here alone.'

He continued to ask questions and soon a queue had formed waiting to speak to me. 'I'll wait for you in the parking area,' he said.

As soon as the people dispersed, I went to meet him. He returned to the question of my family and soon had it out of me that it would take $5000 to bring them from Japan.

'I think my wife and I can give you that.'

I thought I must be dreaming! I muttered some attempt at thanking him, and said that I had never expected this to happen.

'Don't thank me,' he replied. 'If I should die in a car accident on the way home, you would have nothing to thank me for. Just thank God.'

At nine o'clock the following morning, he turned up at Mr. Coon's house and at last I learned his name! Frederick Nymeyer was a Christian Reformed Church layman - a former board member of six big companies and retired economics editor of the *Chicago Sun*. We drove to his home and entered his office. From a desk drawer he took a letter and invited me to read it. It was addressed to his bank: 'Please remit $5000 to the Reformation Translation Fellowship Inc, to be used as travel money to bring the family of Rev. Charles H. Chao to the United States. No written report or public announcement of this gift is to be published by the Reformation Translation Fellowship.' It was signed by himself.

As I read, my heart overflowed with thanksgiving! God had answered my prayer, as it were overnight! I remembered the Seminary's promise of sponsorship should the $5000 be forthcoming and I could only quietly praise God in my heart.

As Mr. Nymeyer later entertained me to a meal in a steak house, I asked him, 'Considering we never met each other before yesterday, how can you make such a generous donation?'

'Three reasons,' he said. 'First, I am strongly

anti-Communist and people like you who have been under such threat need help; second, your beliefs agree totally with my own; and third, I believe that a wife should be with her husband!'

I was deeply moved. This was amazing grace! This was God at work and it was 'marvellous in our eyes'.

From Pastor Coon's home, I phoned Bruce Willson with my news. 'Thank God,' he said, 'for such a quick answer to our prayers. I'll recommend to the Home Missions Board that they help you.'

My preaching tour covered a total of fourteen states. In Kansas, my host was Paul Hindman, pastor of the Associated Presbyterian Church in the small town of Minneola. During the week, Mr. Hindman held a job at the local Post Office. He listened to the story of my family and of the work of the R.T.F. I told him, too, about Mr. Nymeyer's gift.

'Brother Chao,' he said, 'when your family comes to the States, would you like to do Chinese literature work here?' He explained that a house would be available which had recently been vacated by a pastor of their denomination in Arkansas. It was large and in a quiet spot - ideal for my kind of work. Would I like to see it?

It took us two days to travel the several hundred miles with a one-night motel stop. Mrs. Hindman came too and their two sons. American hospitality amazed me. A man I had never met before was willing to stop his work, leave home with his family for several days, drive hundreds of miles - all to show me a house for my family! And his wife didn't complain!

We saw the house and left the matter in the Lord's hands. Ever since, I felt great love and respect for the Hindmans: if I am passing through Minneola, I drop in and spend the night there, sure of being greeted with brotherly enthusiasm.

My itinerary ended on the West Coast. It was a happy opportunity to revisit churches in California where I had been just one year before.

Back in Pittsburgh, Dr. Willson escorted me to the meeting of the Reformed Presbyterian Board of Home Missions and asked them to act as sponsor for me in the matter of applying to the US Government to have my visa status changed from 'student' to 'resident alien'. He also asked that they sponsor my family's immigrations.

Some controversy arose at this point. Members of the Board were aware of the responsibility of putting up the $4000 a year which would be needed to support my family once they did arrive. It was Dr. Willson who spoke out on my behalf. He pointed out that the R.T.F. was paying me half salary and that what was needed was about $2000.

Then he told of how my needs had been so wonderfully supplied to the tune of $5000 in Chicago.

This money, pointed out Dr. Willson, had been donated by a Christian brother in another denomination. 'Mr. Chao is a member of our church. If one half of his needed money was contributed by a member of another church, should we not donate the other half?'

The arguments ceased. It was resolved that the Board chairman be responsible for helping me to apply for change of visa status. I was told to proceed with plans for bringing my family to America.

With my one year in the Pittsburgh Reformed Presbyterian Seminary now over, I completed all the procedures for entry to Westminster Seminary, Philadelphia.

In the meantime, approval came through of my application for change of status. On May 8th, I would have to leave the country to conclude my 'student' status, then re-enter to qualify as a permanent resident. To fulfil these terms, I took a train to Toronto, over the border in Canada, filled out my re-entry papers at the US Consulate there, and returned after four hours in a 'foreign' country with a light step and a 'green card' - my 'resident alien' registration.

## 16

*The one who calls you is faithful and he will do it*
*(1 Thessalonians 5:24)*

Back in Kobe, my family were jubilant when I sent them the good news. On the 17th of August, 1958, they boarded the *President Cleveland* en route to San Francisco.

I had bought a second-hand estate car and, in spite of my lack of experience on American turnpike roads, I set off from Philadelphia to meet my family in California. At a motel in Indiana, I realised that I had no reverse gear: I had failed to keep the transmission topped up with oil. A garage mechanic estimated that repairs would be over $100; but he assured me that I would be able to keep going in forward gear.

This got me to Oakdale, Illinois, where the pastor took the car to a garage and the Covenanter congregation paid the whole bill of $110! I learnt two lessons. One was practical - always check the oil on a long journey! The other was spiritual - Christians should be like my car - able only to go forward, never backwards!

Next stop was Phoenix, Arizona, where I renewed fellowship with Lester Kilpatrick. 'Let me drive you to Los Angeles,' he said, when he heard about my car trouble. It was my third visit to that city. We both stayed at the home of Pastor Paul Robb - 5081 Montezuma Street.

'Charles,' he said one day in his garden, 'if you like, I'll sell you this house when your family arrive.' It was large and Paul, who was still a bachelor, had an elderly housekeeper to look after meals and household chores. An ideal house for my family - but where would I get the kind of money that would be needed to buy it? The matter was dropped.

* * * * * *

Two whole years had passed since I had left Japan. Every day I had committed to God the entire business of our future reunion. Countless letters had been exchanged. How we longed to be reunited!

As I saw them disembark, my heart overflowed with thankfulness. With God, nothing is impossible. I rededicated my life and talents to him that day, vowing to do whatever he might bid me do.

For our children, there was now a much better opportunity for education: Chinese children found it difficult to compete with Japanese.

Here, too, there was less racial prejudice against Chinese. Besides, most of the American people we knew were Christians. All of these reasons had helped me to look to America as our ultimate home if God opened the way. Now we could see that the long winding path had been travelled under his guidance. To him be the glory!

The Los Angeles Reformed Presbyterian Church had found us a house in the downtown area of the city. It was a slowly deteriorating district, racially mixed but predominantly black. Our rented house was owned by a Filipino and the previous tenant had been a Mexican drug-smuggler.

There arrived one day a man from the gas company, as he claimed, to check the gas line in our back yard. Jonathan went with him and stayed there, and he was not able to dig up the hidden heroin buried there; he had been our Mexican friend in disguise. The FBI were informed, but the man never returned.

For about a year I continued a dual ministry of preaching and literature work. But the crime rate was high: there were frequent visits from the FBI to check on this and that; I decided that we should move to a better area. Someone suggested that our $260 a month rent would be better used if we bought; but were where we to acquire cash for the high down-payment?

Then I remembered Mr. Nymeyer in Chicago. I was to write to him, he had said, if any financial problems arose. Off went a letter outlining the house problem; back came another $5000 to the R.T.F.! An elder in the Reformed Presbyterian congregation was assigned to assist me in buying, and our final choice was 5081 Montezuma Street! We moved in on September 1st, 1959, thus bringing to reality what I had taken as a joke by Paul Robb only a year before! Ten years later we were enabled as a family to make the house our very own property.

## 17

## *Fellow-citizens with the saints*
### *(Ephesians 2:19)*

When my wife and I were married in 1932, it never crossed our minds that we would ever leave our ancestral village home in southern Manchuria. That God would take us in his service to Mukden, Peking, Shanghai, Canton, Hong Kong, Japan and finally to America, was beyond our wildest dreams! Now, in the cause of promoting the work of the Reformation Translation Fellowship, airliners were to carry us around the earth to places which we had never heard of in our younger days.

It was with the help of many Christian friends and churches that I took my first world tour in 1967. In a ten-week spell in the spring of that year, I visited Chinese churches and missions in Japan and Taiwan, the Philippines, Burma and India, Lebanon and Israel, and the major cities of Western Europe, including brief stops in Belgium and the British Isles. In Taiwan I renewed friendships made in 1965 at the time of my first visit there for the wedding of Jonathan and Rebecca.

Jonathan was teaching there and had become well acquainted with Christian leaders. For two years before his marriage, he had assumed temporary direction of the R.T.F. work in Taiwan, looking after the finances and seeing to the distribution of *Faith and Life*. It was his suggestion that the R.T.F. office be moved to Taipei instead of our trying to operate it from Los Angeles and Hong Kong. By 1968, the American Board of the R.T.F. had officially authorised the move.

Suitable living and working accommodation was found and in June my wife and I after spending the summer in Los Angeles moved to Taipei with our youngest daughters, Lois and Rose. Within two years, they too had gone to America to pursue their studies, and from that time we had to maintain a home in Taipei and a home in Los Angeles. Travel between the two became a way of life; if it had not been for the substantial help of our daughter, Helen, a stewardess with Pan-Am, and the customary reduced fares for employees' parents, such long flights would have been impossible.

\* \* \* \* \* \*

1976 was the year of my deputation tour which was to take me across the USA, into Canada and overseas to Britain, New Zealand and Australia. Again the whole thing was made possible by the efforts and help of many people who co-ordinated our plans and ensured a successful tour.

We began on August 12th at a meeting of the R.T.F. held during the Reformed Presbyterian Synod. Here it was decided that the next year we should translate and publish J.G. Vos' lectures on the Book of Revelation. Thereafter we were privileged to meet with congregations who, I knew, generously supported our work.

It was an opportunity, too, to meet up with old friends and to make new friends in the Lord. An elder in a Kansas church drove me to Rock Port, Missouri, to meet once again Dr. Loraine Boettner, a man of God in whose footsteps I feel compelled to follow: a quietly effective servant of the Lord, he seeking only to propagate Bible truth.

In Pittsburgh I was able to visit our dear friend of Kobe days, Miss Rose Huston, who resided in the Reformed Presbyterian Aged People's Home. She it was who had been so sympathetic of the needs of our large family - and had started us off in our egg-sales! In Illinois I visited my generous Christian friends, the Nymeyers, who did so much for the R.T.F. In Grand Rapids, Michigan, I received much kindness at the hands of Mr. and Mrs. Kuiper. Mr. Kuiper had been sending me tapes of lectures and sermons by Reformed ministers. They gifted many books to me in Taiwan.

Rev. Wing Mak is a pastor of the United Church in Ottawa. There is an encouraging work among the Chinese in the Canadian capital. Rev. Mak it was who suggested that R.T.F. translate Dr. Packer's *Knowing God*.

At the end of October I found myself in Scotland where I received great encouragement and generous gifts from Christian friends. My visit was arranged by Rev. Sinclair Horne of the Scottish Reformation Society and John J. Murray, then British secretary (now chairman) of the R.T.F. The Free Church of Scotland and the Free Presbyterian Church invited me to present the work of the R.T.F. in Glasgow, Inverness, Perth and Edinburgh. At Inverness, we were delighted to meet Mrs. Tallach, the mother of our friend, Dr. Cameron Tallach, who worked at the Christian Clinic in Taipei before moving to Hong Kong.

I felt somewhat uneasy in Belfast, Northern Ireland, where we flew with Mr. Horne as our guide. It is a land of much internal strife, although no violence took place while we were there. But these Irish churches are so generous to the R.T.F. and what wonderful fellowship I enjoyed with those Irish pastors.

In London, I addressed three hundred at the Chinese Christian Church and was gratified to learn that groups such as these are flourishing.

After a public meeting in Westminster Chapel, a stranger approached me and talked about translation work in China. Before we parted, he graciously donated £300 to the work!

In mid-November, we set out for new ground - New Zealand and Australia.

In Auckland we were met by Rev. George Mackenzie and Bill van Rij. Mr. Van Rij was manager of General Foods Corporation in New Zealand and it was he who had invited us to visit the Southern Hemisphere. He was a reader of the *Banner of Truth* magazine and had read there about the R.T.F. Through John J. Murray he had learned of our work in Taipei. Now here we were, fulfilling that invitation.

It was Rev. Mackenzie who was so kind and whose efforts were so noble when we ran into visa problems the day we were to fly to Australia. Much time was lost in satisfying Australian entry requirements and we missed our plane. Another airline had to be taken and my concession tickets were not valid. It was the kind people of Mackenzie's congregation who contributed money towards our air fares to Sydney.

We remember with gratitude the generous gifts to the R.T.F. from the Ryde Reformed Presbyterian Church, who were small in numbers but big in heart. Tasmania, we found, has several small congregations which are nevertheless strong in the Reformed Faith.

On 16th December we touched down again at Taipei to be met by Sam, teaching at the Christian College and Bill, back to Taiwan for a visit after graduating from the University of California in Los Angeles. We had so much to be thankful for and to rejoice about as we thought back on the wonderful Christian support in the Southern Hemisphere, and God's marvellous protection and grace during our travels.

* * * * * *

1977 was a special year for us. In February, a letter arrived in Taiwan for me from Dr. Edwin Clarke, President of Geneva College. It said that I had been selected as a candidate for the honorary degree of Doctor of Divinity.

At the end of April we had a reunion with our children in Los Angeles. Then it was on to Atlantic City and Philadelphia. On the way, we stopped at Pittsburgh to visit Rose Huston, little thinking it was the last time we would be seeing her: she died two years later.

On the 10th of May, we were at Geneva College amid much picture-taking, and surrounded by family and friends. Samuel E. Boyle was there, as was Lester Kilpatrick. It was our dear friend and my teacher, Dr. J.G. Vos, who presented me and read the following citation full of gracious compliments before placing the academic hood around me.

President Clarke, it is my pleasure and my privilege to present for the conferring of an honorary degree the Reverend Charles Chung-hui, my one-time colleague in Christian work in Manchuria, my friend and brother in Christ, a man who has been greatly used by the Lord in the defence and promotion of the Reformed Faith, or consistent Biblical Christianity, among the people of China.

During the years of World War II Mr. Chao continued his work in Manchuria with true fortitude in spite of constant danger of arrest, imprisonment, torture and even death at the hands of Japanese military occupation authorities in Manchuria. At the end of World War II, by a series of amazing dispensations of divine providence, he and his family were able to escape the advancing tide of Communism, both Russian and Chinese, which made Christian witness in Manchuria virtually impossible. He lived successively in Canton, the Crown Colony of Hong Kong, Japan, and for a time in California, and finally now in Taiwan in 'Free China'.

From 1949, in collaboration with the Rev. Samuel E. Boyle and others he was Executive Secretary of the Reformation Fellowship, an organisation to provide sound Christian religious and theological literature in the Chinese language. As Mr. Boyle and his colleagues recognised, there was a great lack of such literature available. Much of what was available was superficial and vitiated by unsound teaching.

Mr. Chao edited the Chinese quarterly *Reformed Faith and Life* magazine, which has been published regularly for the past 27 years. For some years it was possible to transmit this periodical and other materials inside of Communist China through the mails, but later it became impossible. However, the magazine and other materials continue to be circulated among the many millions of Chinese in Taiwan and other countries of the Pacific areas. The numerous responses from readers have shown that this material is read and appreciated by those who read it.

Mr. Chao received his A.B. degree from Kwansei Gakuin University in Japan in 1956. Later he studied at the Reformed Presbyterian Theological Seminary in Pittsburgh, and at Westminster Theological Seminary, Philadelphia. He was ordained to the gospel ministry by the Reformed Presbyterian Church of North America in Japan in 1954.

Mr. Chao's works of translation and original writing in Chinese are too numerous to mention in detail in this citation. In collaboration with the Rev. Samuel E. Boyle he translated Dr. J. Gresham Machen's classic *Christianity and Liberalism*. Other important works translated by Mr. Chao include: Benjamin B. Warfield, *Calvin as a Theologian and Calvinism Today*; Oswald T. Allis, *God Spake by Moses*; *The Westminster Confession of Faith*; James I. Packer, *Evangelism and the Sovereignty of God*; John Calvin, *Commentary on the Epistle to the Romans*; Harvie M. Conn, *Contemporary World Theology*; Louis Berkhof, *Manual of Christian Doctrine*. Besides these major works, a great many shorter articles, booklets and tracts have been authored or translated by Mr. Chao, and published by the Reformation Translation Fellowship widely through the Pacific area.

Mr. and Mrs. Chao have ten children. Two of the sons, Theodore and Jonathan, are Geneva College graduates. The escape of Mrs. Chao and children to join her husband, as they fled from before the Communist peril was a divine providence that seems almost miraculous. By the singular blessing of God the whole family escaped from Communist Manchuria to parts of China that were temporarily free.

President Clarke, for all these reasons and others which could be mentioned, I have the honour to present the Rev. Charles Chung-hui for the degree of Doctor of Divinity *honoris causa*.



It was an emotional moment. I thought of how life had begun for me in far-away Manchuria in a poor and insignificant family and of the kindness of countless people along the way who had helped me because of the love of our Lord Jesus. I was conscious that day of my own unworthiness and of the grace of Almighty God.

## 18

*Even in your old age...I am he...*
*who will sustain you.*
(Isaiah 46:4)

In 1977 we had two changes of house - one in California and one in Taiwan. Apart from the fact that our old Highland Park house was deteriorating, we began to be troubled by neighbours and were the victims of vandalism and petty theft. Our daughter Rose suggested a move and by God's providence we found another place in Temple City where things were much better. Through our friend, Rev. Po, we found a suitable home in Taipei after our landlord decided to sell the property we were in, and there we have lived ever since.

That year too, our third son Sam was married in Taipei to Lorna. Lorna was born in Vietnam and came to Taiwan a the age of six. She had been secretary to the President of Chungyun Christian University. A the time of writing, Sam is working for his Ph.D at Fuller Theological Seminary while Lorna is secretary of a Chinese translation society who have done work on books by Dr. G Campbell

Morgan. Since then, daughter Rose has married Albert Lee, an American of Cantonese descent who practises as a paediatrician. Our bachelor son Harry is always our host these days when we have our annual spell in the United States. Trained in Belgium, he is now doing well as a doctor at a medical clinic in California.

1982 was the year of our youngest son Bill's marriage to Carol Hsi, and July 10th of that year was a big day for Pearl and me: it was our Golden Wedding, and we celebrated it surrounded by our children.

\* \* \* \* \* \*

So much for ourselves and the family. What of the translation work and the RTF?

Through the efforts of G.M.W. Spear, a missionary of the Reformed Presbyterian Church of North America in Japan, the RTF Japan Board was established in 1978. We thank God for the financial support we receive from time to time from this band of Japanese people of Reformed outlook.

That year I was kept busy on several literary projects and was enabled to translate a number of important books into Chinese as well as to see them through the various stages leading to final publication. In the autumn of the year and with the permission of Mr. G. I. Williamson and the Presbyterian and Reformed Publishing Company of Phillipsbury, New Jersey, I arranged for the translation of his study of the Shorter Catechism. I was teaching a class at a graduate school of theology in Hong Kong at the time; the material was divided into parts and translated by the students.

The autumn of 1979 saw me on deputation work in Japan where I was able to visit various Reformed congregations and to thank them for their support. I was invited to address the Senate of Kobe Reformed Theological Seminary; my old friend of student days, Mr. Hashimoto, is President there. I had a wonderful time, too, with Rev. Ichiro Akishege at Nagoya. I first met him during my Seminary days in Manchuria; he helped us as an interpreter with the Japanese military authorities when Newchang was closed during Dr. Vos' time there.

The last time I saw Dr. Vos was during my 1981 trip to our Senate meeting. He was then in the Reformed Presbyterian Home. On the same trip I had happy reunions with my friends Dr. Loraine Boettner and the Boyles to whom Dr. Vos had introduced me in the early days. Sadly, two year later, in June 1983, I was to find myself leading in prayer at Dr. Vos' funeral in Kansas. God in his goodness had led me to be Dr. Vos' student, friend and latterly co-worker. I owe much to him. At the Senate meeting itself, the Foreign Mission Board of the R.P. Church of North America decided that I be 'loaned' to the R.T.F. as a missionary working in Taiwan. This was the highlight of the year for me - to be put on the payroll of the Foreign Mission Board.

\* \* \* \* \* \*

The autumn of 1983 took me to Britain and Holland. All arrangements in Holland were made by Mrs. Mijndern, President of the Mission Organisation there. I spoke at meetings in St Annaland, Montfoort and Rotterdam where the congregations adhere to the Reformed faith and are generous in their contributions to the RTF.

My companions on the Holland trip were Rev. John J. Murray, then Secretary of the British RTF, and Mr. Jan Van Voerden whose wife is Scottish and who has a church in Scotland. Mr. Van Voerden acted as my interpreter. In Scotland, we had a meeting of the British RTF at which it was agreed to give financial support with the publication of material already translated and prepared. These were Berkhof's *Manual of Christian Doctrine* and B.B. Warfield's booklet *Calvin as a Theologian and Calvinism Today*.

It was my son Jonathan who first suggested that

I translate Herman Bavinck's *A Reasonable Faith,* one of the most concise presentations of the Reformed stand-point. I started out on the work in faith in 1987, without knowing where the money was to come from if it was ever to be published. The next year Jonathan went to Holland to speak again to our friends in the Reformed congregations and let it be known that I was at work on Bavinck's book. I had a wonderful surprise when he returned. He called me long distance from Hong Kong.

'Dad,' he said, 'good news: our friends in Holland have given $9000 for the publication of *A Reasonable Faith.*'

What a wonderful provider our God is!

And he made another similar provision for us. In 1983 I had met Mr. Simon Box, church news editor of the *Reformed Daily News* in Holland. He had interviewed me on that occasion and I had had the chance to testify to the active church work going on in Taiwan and had told him also about our own R.T.F. Mr. Box visited mainland China and Taiwan in 1990. This time I told him about my *Dictionary of Theological Terms,* started in 1983 and regularly checked and enlarged. Through the readers of Mr. Box's paper in Holland, $25,000 was raised and given to the RTF for publication of the latest edition of the dictionary. It was published, praise God, at the end of 1990. Besides that, Mr. Box has undertaken to be RTF representative in Holland.

\* \* \* \* \* \*

One of my trips to Holland was the origin of another memorable experience.

In the course of my addresses, I made mention of the man who was instrumental in my conversion in 1935 - Mr. Wang Ming Tao.

Mr. Wang had spent over twenty-two years in Communist prisons in Peking and elsewhere. At the end of 1979, the People's Republic of China was recognised by the United States during the Carter administration. Although we do not know whose influence prevailed, whether that of Western friends or others, the order was given to release Mr. Wang. But Mr. Wang gave the prison governor a hard time, refusing to accept release until an official government reason was given why he had been jailed in the first place. The governor, not wanting any complications, sent a telegram to Mr. Wang's son, working at that time for a Chinese scientific organisation. The son went to Shanhsi immediately.

'What are you doing here?' his father asked.

'Didn't you send me a telegram?'

'No.'

'Anyway,' said the son, 'you can get ready to leave. We're going back to Shanghai.'

But Mr. Wang held out, refusing to budge until official government notice came.

Finally, in desperation, the governor removed him to quarters outside the actual prison where, as Mr. Wang told us, he had to do with something less refined than the flushing toilet he had been accustomed to! This made him relent in the end and he sent a message to his son to come for him.

* * * * * *

All this I learned about my dear friend because Mrs. Mijndern, when she heard that I knew Mr. Wang, arranged for me to visit him in 1980. He told us his story of Communist cruelty. He had preached the Gospel powerfully in almost every province on the Chinese mainland and for his efforts had spent those twenty-two years locked up. Even after his release, a Communist agent would make regular visits to ask about how many visitors he had and who they were.

A Baptist writer in Taipei has published seven volumes of all Mr. Wang's writings, so clearly his great influence will always be felt.

Before I left Mr. Wang at the end of that wonderful reunion, we prayed together, and while he prayed, I was conscious of the tears running down my face as I thought of all this great man of God had been through.

* * * * * * *

For some years now, as I have said, I have been spending eight months here in Taipei and four in the United States. Most of my time is taken up with translating and preparing material for our quarterly magazine *Reformed Faith and Life*. The organisation is a small one and the personnel are few - one secretary and sometimes a few friends we may ask, to undertake translating assignments. In May each year we return to the States to be at our church Senate, do some deputation work, see the family - a kind of working holiday.

But now I have reached the age of retirement, and I see the need to find a capable younger man to take my place as Executive Secretary of the R.T.F.

We have already had disappointments in this respect. Two likely young men showed interest in the work at different times, but in each case they went to the States to study theology and then felt unable to take up R.T.F. work afterwards.

At the moment a Taiwan Local Board is planned and we can only hope that an Executive Secretary will be produced from it. He will have to be a man who has real faith in Christ, a man not afraid to lean entirely on the Lord for help.

What we do know is that our God who started this work in 1949 and who has seen it through to the present day will also assuredly make provision when the time comes.

# List of books translated into Chinese by Dr. Chao
(with years of publication)

## 1950

*Karl Marx or Jesus Christ?* V. Raymond Edman (with Samuel E.Boyle)

## 1952

*The Reformed Doctrine of Predestination* Loraine Boettner (reprinted 1970,1975, 1980)

## 1955

*Calvin as a Theologian and Calvinism Today* B.B. Warfield (reprinted 1967, 1984)

## 1956

*A Word to Parents* A.W. Pink (reprinted 1983)
*The Real Meaning of the Reformation* J.G. Vos
*God Spake By Moses* Oswald T. Allis

## 1957

*The Visible Church* J.G. Vos (reprinted 1972)

## 1959

*Why I Believe in God?* Cornelius Van Til (reprinted 1965,1975, 1985)
*The Atonement* Loraine Boettner (reprinted 1988)
*The Spirit of Grace and of Supplications* J. R. Anderson

**1960**

*Christianity Rightly So Called*   Samuel G. Craig

**1962**

*Immortality*   Loraine Boettner (reprinted 1973)

**1963**

*The Meaning of the Word 'Blood' in Scripture*   A.M. Stibbs

**1964**

*Revival Year Sermons*   Charles H. Spurgeon

**1966**

*The End of the Ages*   J.G. Vos  (reprinted 1975)
*The Facts of Christianity*   Samuel E. Boyle
*God, Man and Religion*   J.G. Vos (reprinted 1981)
*Inspiration of the Scriptures*   Loraine Boettner

**1967**

*God's Plan and Man's Destiny*   V.M. Cameron
*Have You Considered Him?*   Wilbur M. Smith

**1968**

*The Prodigal Son*   A.W. Pink
*The Westminster Confession of Faith*   (reprinted 1972, 1981)
*Evangelism and the Sovereignty of God*   J.I. Packer (reprinted 1972, 1987)
*Election*   Charles H. Spurgeon

**1969**

*Tests of Eternal Life*   H.W. Butt

**1970**

*Words to Winners of Souls*  Horatius Bonar

**1971**

*Christian Supernaturalism*  Loraine Boettner
*Commentary on Romans*  John Calvin (reprinted 1978)
(with Watson Soong)
*The Place of the Bible in Modern Theology*  F.S. Leahy

**1972**

*The Trinity*  Loraine Boettner

**1973**

*A Christian Introduction to the Religions of the World*  J.G. Vos  (reprinted 1981)
*World Contemporary Theology*  Harvie M. Conn (reprinted 1979)

**1974**

*Manual of Christian Doctrine*  Louis Berkhof
(with Watson Soong)
*The Five Points of Calvinism*  D.N. Steele and Curtis C. Thomas  (reprinted 1983)
*The Baptism and Fullness of the Holy Spirit*  John R.W. Stott  (reprinted 1986)

**1975**

*The Grace of God in the Gospel*  John Cheesman,
(with David C. Kao)
*Studies in the Book of Genesis*  J.G. Vos (reprinted 1988)

## 1976

*Westminster Shorter Catechism* (reprinted 1978, 1982)

## 1977

*What is Original Sin?* J.G. Machen
*The Good Hope of the Life Everlasting* W. MacLean

## 1978

*Studies in the Book of Revelation* J.G. Vos

## 1979

*The Person of Christ* Loraine Boettner

## 1980

*What Am I?* G.W. Spear
*The Bible Tells Us So* R B. Kuiper

## 1981

*What is Christian Education?* J.G. Vos

## 1982

*Studies in the Epistle to the Romans* J.G. Vos
*John Calvin's Devotions and Prayers*

## 1983

*The Charismatics: A Doctrinal Perspective* J.F. MacArthur

## 1984

*The History of Christian Doctrine* Louis Berkhof
*Into Life* Philip Doddridge

## 1985

*The Reformed Faith* Loraine Boettner
*Grace Abounding* John Bunyan
*A Message to Preachers and Other Essays* A.W. Pink

*Who is in Control?*   A.W. Pink
(with Jack Lee)
*Golden Booklet of the True Christian Life*   John Calvin

**1986**
*In the Beginning*   E. J. Young
*The Millennium*   Loraine Boettner
**1989**
*Our Reasonable Faith*   Herman Bavinick

**Books written by
Dr. Chao
for Chinese readers.**

**1967**
*A Bird's Eye View Study of the Bible*   (reprinted 1981)

**1972**
*Christian Fundamentals and Modern Theological Thought*   (reprinted 1979)

**1983**
*His Grace Abounding*   Charles Chao's Autobiography
*A New Practical Dictionary of Theological Terms*